"WHERE GOD PUT THE WEST"

Movie Making in the Desert

by

Bette L. Stanton

John Wayne on location in southeastern Utah

A Moab – Monument Valley Movie History

Dedicated to the late

GEORGE E. WHITE

> Founder of the Moab Movie Committee, whose unyielding dedication kept film companies coming to southeastern Utah for over four decades.

and to the late

HARRY GOULDING

> Who pioneered filmmaking in Monument Valley, bringing its magnificent landscape to the attention of the world.

In honor of the Moab to
Monument Valley Film
Commission, the longest
ongoing film commission
in the World.

iii

Second edition
Copyright © 1994

Published by Canyonlands Natural History Association,
3031 South Highway 191, Moab, Utah 84532.

Printed and bound in the United States of America

Editors: Jeanie Reynolds, Cheryl East, Camilla Greene, John and
Nancy Hauer, Ber and Charlotte Knight and Vicki Barker.

Special Consultants: The late George E. White and the late Leone
"Mike" Goulding.

Library of Congress Cataloging-in-Publication Data:

Stanton, Bette L. (Bette Larsen)
    "Where God Put the West"

A Moab-Monument Valley Movie History

    First published (c 1993) by Four Corners Publication, Moab, Utah.

    ISBN: 0-937407-08-9

For information on future updated printing contact: Bette L. Stanton
P.O. Box 61, Moab, Utah 84532, or Canyonlands Natural History
Association, 3031 South Highway 191, Moab, Utah 84532.

Cover photo: John Wayne leading cavalry in scene from *Rio Grande,*
on location in Professor Valley near Moab, Utah.

Dedication pages: Scene from *She Wore A Yellow Ribbon,*
filmed in Monument Valley.

Rio Conchos, 1964. During the 1950's and 60's it was not uncommon for movie companies to build elaborate sets at a location miles from civilization. This set was located in Professor Valley, 22 miles northeast of Moab. The building was burned in the movie and all that remains are the rock steps that led to the front porch. Photo by Lin Ottinger.

ACKNOWLEDGEMENTS

The film industry has given southeastern Utah history a dose of unexpected glamour. Area visitors and new residents are often unaware of the enchanting Hollywood past throughout this high desert plateau. After four and a half decades of filmmaking in Moab and nearly seven decades of film production in Monument Valley, many citizens have stepped forward to help document this important aspect of canyon country's legacy.

Those who have shared their memories and photographs include: George and Mary Esther White, "Mike" Goulding, Essie White, Manuel "Bud" Lincoln, Lin Ottinger, Arnel Holyoak, Jack Goodspeed, Rusty Musselman, Virginia Johnson, Roberta Knutson, Barbara Burck Cathey, Lucille Carlisle, Gloria Harris, Ev and Betty Schumaker, Winford Bunce, Karl Tangren, Mitch and Mary Williams, Dixie Barker Barksdale, Sheri Griffith, Pete Plastow, Dennis Sweeney, Glen Victor, Don Swasey, Kyle Bailey, Ken Sleight, Don Holyoak, Ron Griffith, Bego Gerhart, Larry Campbell, Joe Kingsley, Bonnie Midlam, Ralph Miller, Patsy Allred, Ray Tibbetts, Tony Osusky, Veldon McKinnon, John Hagner, Eric Bjornstad, Mary von Koch, B.J. Griffith, Rock Smith, Peggy Humphreys, Lloyd Pierson, Art Manzanares, Les Rogers, Glenna White Thomas, Clyde Gonzales, Clea Johnson, Lynn Stones, Cindi Stevenson and Davina Smith. Their efforts have been deeply appreciated.

Gathering the material for this publication has taken several years. While space will not allow a complete list of all those who helped, individuals who assisted with researching printed material, photo searches, interviewing participants, and compiling this book include: Dorothy Larsen, Robbie Swasey, Marian Eason, Kari Murphy, Tyde Stanton, Yvonne Pierson, Renee Wallis, Tina Lopez, Dina McCandless, Eileen Leech and Mary Engleman.

A special thanks goes to *The Times-Independent*, whose vintage stories over the decades contributed greatly to this publication. Co-editors/publishers Sam and Adrien Taylor have been a valuable resource throughout this endeavor.

Carlo Gaberscek, author and specialist on Western movie classics, of Undine, Italy; James D'Arc, archives curator, Brigham Young University; Leigh von der Esch, Director of the Utah State Film Commission; and the entire Moab to Monument Valley Film Commission also deserve thanks for their encouragement and assistance.

Foremost, a grateful thank you goes to Bradley Morrison, without whom this history would not have been printed.

Delicate Arch, used in many logos to promote Utah's canyon country, has become a world famous trademark. Located in Arches National Park, it can now be seen on Utah's Centennial license plates. Delicate Arch is a popular film location for television commercials and ad campaigns. Courtesy of the Grand County Travel Council.

CONTENTS

*Scene from the movie, **Blue**. Photo by Lin Ottinger.*

All photographs and illustrations courtesy of the Moab to Monument Valley Film Commission unless otherwise credited.

Sunrise over "John Ford Country" in Monument Valley, Utah, taken from Goulding's Lodge.

*Artist rendering of set designed for John Wayne movie **The Comancheros**, filmed in Professor Valley near Moab, Utah. Courtesy of George White.*

"WHERE GOD PUT THE WEST"

TV you can make on the backlot, but for the big screen, for the real outdoor dramas, you have to do it where God put the West...and there is no better example of this than around Moab.

John Wayne

INTRODUCTION

John Wayne was well acquainted with southeastern Utah when he made this remark in 1961, while filming **The Comancheros**. It was the 1939 movie **Stagecoach**, shot in Monument Valley, that brought the "Duke" his first recognition as a major star.

While Wayne went on to acquire a world-wide image as *the* Western hero, it was director John Ford who turned Westerns into film classics. He brought Moab-Monument Valley landscapes to the screen in such forceful images that the region became known in Hollywood as "John Ford Country." From 1938 to 1961, Ford directed nine movies in the area. His superb use of vast desert panoramas had the effect of discouraging other directors from trespassing, although a few, such as George Sherman, Gordon Douglas, Edward Dmytryk, and Blake Edwards, couldn't resist this spectacular land for scenes in their own films. Later, as the popularity of Westerns declined, Moab and Monument Valley were largely forgotten by Hollywood. Only in recent years have producers and directors rediscovered the versatile beauty of southeastern Utah for other scenarios, such as galactic and contemporary adventure. It was the unique formations of Arches National Park that attracted director Steven Spielberg to Moab to film the opening scenes for **Indiana Jones and the Last Crusade** in 1988.

It takes a special breed of people to make movie magic in the desert. Sets must be built miles from civilization. The logistics involving transportation, livestock, and extras take on a new complexity in rugged terrain and often extreme temperatures. But the scenery in Utah's canyon country keeps filmmakers coming. Director Ridley Scott, while searching locations for **Thelma and Louise** in 1989, remarked after his first day out: "I have seen more wonderful and varied scenery in a single day around Moab than any other day I have ever scouted."

The list of stars and producers who have made Moab and Monument Valley their temporary homes reads like "Who's Who in Hollywood." While this is a story of celebrities and the cinema, it is also about the residents in a special section of rural America who have supported movie making for more than six decades. Real-life cowboys and Indians, miners, ranch wives, townspeople, and schoolchildren are included; this is no less their story.

NATURE'S PHENOMENAL BACKDROPS

Volumes have been written about Hollywood, the major studios and the celebrities who have made up this glamorous industry, yet little can be found that describes the great outdoor locations that lured producers away from their studio empires.

Along the southeastern borders of Utah, nature has carved an abundance of backdrops that could never be duplicated in a studio backlot. Rising out of the desert are great mesas, buttes, sandstone pinnacles, spires, fins and arches, all monuments to 500 million years of gigantic earth uplifts and the perpetual forces of erosion. These towering formations captivate the imagination with their immensity and timelessness.

In addition to the unbelievable selection of settings offered in canyon country, directors and cinematographers have a wide spectrum of color from which to choose. Terra cotta rocks that cast black shadows in the brilliant desert sun glow like they're on fire in late afternoon...endless cerulean skies broken only by a few white cumulus puffs...a desert palette of the most subtle blues, greens, purple, grays and tans imaginable: all are found in abundance in southeastern Utah.

Determination Towers in Mill Canyon, northwest of Moab.

Beaver Lake in the La Sal Mountains, southeast of Moab and northeast of Monticello, Utah.

2

Colorado River as seen from the Moab Rim off Kane Creek road. Photo by Dan Mick.

The Monitor and the Merrimac buttes, from Highway 313.

Ken's Lake, nine miles southeast of Moab, with red rock cliffs and the La Sal Mountains in the background.

Vista of Behind the Rocks area and La Sal Mountains, from Pucker Pass at head of Long Canyon.

State Highway 313. Photo by Ron Griffith.

Wild Horse Canyon near Goblin Valley State Park.

The Navajo Twins overlooking Bluff, Utah.

Onion Creek Canyon in Professor Valley.

The highway through Courthouse Towers in Arches National Park is popular for filming car commercials.

Former Secretary of the Interior Stewart Udall described this area as "acre for acre, the most beautiful country in the world."

The region, which encompasses San Juan and Grand counties, covers 11,576 square miles. It is sparsely settled, with a population of only 20,000 or 1.7 persons per square mile. Four rivers snake their way through this high desert landscape: the Green, Dolores, San Juan and mighty Colorado. The elevation varies from 4,000 feet above sea level to nearly 13,000 feet, with the second highest mountain range in the state of Utah. Easily accessible, the changing scenery often stretches for miles with no fences, power lines, highways, or other traces of civilization within view.

North Mitten in Monument Valley. The Utah-Arizona line cuts between the North and South Mittens.

5

View from Dead Horse Point State Park.
Courtesy of Grand County Travel Council.

THE PROMOTERS

The Oldest, Ongoing Film Commission

HOW IT ALL BEGAN

It has often been said that director John Ford "discovered" Monument Valley. Some authors credit John Wayne with finding the area and bringing it to Ford's attention. Actually, it was director George B. Seitz who first called "Lights! Camera! Action!" in the land of the monuments, when he filmed *The Vanishing American* in 1925. But it was Harry Goulding who, in 1938, brought the film industry to stay in southeastern Utah.

Goulding first visited Monument Valley in the early 1920s when the only way into the area was on foot or horseback. Captivated by this enchanting land, he hoped someday to make it his home. During his early trips to the valley he helped the Navajo Indians prevent a "shooting war" with neighboring Paiutes. In gratitude, the Navajos allowed him to homestead a small piece of reservation land "slap dab amongst the monuments."

With a new bride nicknamed "Mike" and a few sheep, Goulding settled in and built a small trading post at the base of Big Rock Door Mesa. His was the only land privately held by a non-Indian in the 25,000 square mile reservation that straddles three of the Four Corners states.

As the 1930s Depression took its toll across the country, nowhere was poverty so stark a reality as in the Navajo Nation. The Gouldings knew the situation was desperate. As a possible solution, Harry decided to sell the area's most valuable commodity - its spectacular scenery. His goal was to convince Hollywood to film a movie in Monument Valley.

Filming on location was rare in those days. The movie moguls, with their big studios and backlots, kept most business close to home. On the rare occasions when movie companies did travel outside California for filming, their choice was often Kanab, Utah, known in the 1930s and 1940s as "Little Hollywood." The Gouldings had witnessed the economic boost the film industry had given Kanab. Not only were big bucks brought in by the production companies, but movie making also attracted hundreds of tourists each year.

Mike Goulding's brother in California advised Harry that United Artists Studio was planning to film a Western. It was a hot lead, just what Harry needed. Josef Muench, noted Arizona Highways photographer and friend of the Gouldings, suggested that Harry take photographs along to help sell his "backyard." Josef and his wife, Joyce, prepared 24 black and white photos for the trip. Armed with these, a bedroll and their last $60, the Gouldings headed for Hollywood.

Harry Goulding's tenacity got him through the first door at United Artists and, as interest accelerated, he was introduced on up the line. Eventually, John Ford and Walter Wanger, production chief of United Artists, joined the group.

Though fascinated with Goulding's photos and descriptions of Monument Valley, production officials had grave doubts about the feasibility of filming their project in such a remote area. In the first place, the only accommodations in this wilderness consisted of Goulding's Trading Post and a few stone cabins. Second, and most critical, production of their new Western was to begin in three days. How could Goulding possibly prepare to handle a crew of 100 in such a short time? "The first thing you have to learn," Wanger explained to Goulding, "is that when Hollywood wants to do something right now, they do it *right now*."

Following hours of deliberation, the moviemakers decided to take the risk. Sold on Monument Valley and betting on the unyielding grit of Harry Goulding, they issued him a check and sent him home to prepare for the Hollywood invasion. The product of this challenging venture was the 1939 release of the feature *Stagecoach*, the first and perhaps greatest Western classic ever produced. It was destined to make Monument Valley synonymous with "the Old West."

Harry Goulding in Monument Valley, 1940s.

The 1940s brought nearly a decade of war and its aftermath. During these troubled times, Hollywood's larger-than-life celebrities bolstered morale by performing live for front-line troops. Magazine stands were flooded with movie publications, and major stars of the era became familiar names in every household.

Through all of this, film crews continued their trek to Monument Valley, providing much needed work for the Navajos. Features produced during the forties include *Kit Carson, Billy The Kid, The Harvey Girls, My Darling Clementine, Fort Apache,* and *She Wore A Yellow Ribbon.* The last three were directed by John Ford.

7

Tent City set up during early years of filming in Monument Valley. Courtesy of the Academy of Motion Picture Arts and Sciences.

MOAB DISCOVERED

By the close of the decade, the Television Academy of Arts and Sciences had awarded its first "Emmy," and Hollywood was feeling the threat of the television industry. It was 1949 and John Ford had just completed filming his fourth picture in Monument Valley and was looking for a change of scenery. Someone suggested that he consider the magnificent landscapes surrounding Moab, Utah. With a new movie scheduled for production almost immediately, he was eager to scout the area.

Upon his arrival in Moab, John Ford went straight to the office of L.L. "Bish" Taylor, editor/ publisher of *The Times-Independent* newspaper. Taylor was quick to see the economic potential of the film industry for his community. To get the ball rolling, he introduced Ford to his good friend, George White.

George and his wife, Essie, owned a cattle ranch in a scenic setting beside the Colorado River. George also worked for the state road department and knew the country well. Ford discussed his next movie, **Wagon Master,** and asked White to help find the required film locations.

White concluded that Professor Valley offered everything needed in the script. For a panoramic view of the valley, George took Ford out on a gravel bar at Nine Mile Bottom on the Colorado River. Looking downriver past Fisher Towers and the Priest and the Nuns butte, with the La Sal Mountains as backdrop, Ford exclaimed, "That's the greatest sight I've ever seen!" and declared the production a "go" for Moab.

George White was asked to get things organized for the Hollywood onslaught. Transportation, drivers, livestock and wranglers had to be arranged. Lodging had to be found for 100 crew members, plus the many Native Americans to be used in the picture. And the list went on.

George White, Moab movie committee founder.

At that time, Moab had only a few more accommodations than Monument Valley. The major lodge in town was the Utah Motel, (replaced by today's Best Western Canyonlands Motel). A few cabins existed here and there, such as those connected with Fern's Cafe and Tavern (now the Bowen Motel), but to meet demands, it was necessary to improvise.

Some of the stars and production officials were placed in private homes. To house part of the crew, a tent city was erected behind Farrer's Grocery, at First North and Main Street (now the Poplar Place restaurant). Camps for the Indians were set up by the river bridge (now Lions Club Park), and on Kerby's property (present city park and pool).

8

The film company rented Arches Cafe, in what is now the Energy Building, and arrangements were made with owners Stan and Ruth Peck to handle all in-town meals for the crew. Anderson's Catering, a California-based operation, served the meals on location.

Ford's company, Argosy Productions, employed nearly all of Moab's 1,200 residents. Although it was an economic godsend to a town that had never quite recovered from the Great Depression, there were problems.

About two weeks into production on **Wagon Master**, John Ford gathered all the drivers and wranglers and advised them to "go union" or be replaced with union people from other areas. His picture was union, and Utah was not yet a "right-to-work" state. William Fracnell, head of the Teamsters Local 222 out of Salt Lake City, was called in to meet with local men and show them how to organize. Cap Maxwell, Johnnie Johnson, Arnel and Ray Holyoak, Jack Goodspeed, Ralph Dalton, and Earl Sommerville were among those present. In those days, it cost $75 to join the Union, with $5 per month dues. This met with some resistance, but since the going wage in Moab averaged .75 per hour, and union wages were $1.95 per hour, attitudes soon softened and the union had new members.

MOVIE COMMITTEE FORMED

Almost immediately, George White recognized the need for a movie committee. Schedules had to be coordinated and arrangements made for the required goods and services. Arbitrators were needed to resolve problems during production and Union 399, as well as the Local 222, had to be dealt with. If the movie business was to become a part of Moab's future, citizens needed to learn more about the industry. To keep Hollywood coming to Moab, promotion within the film industry would be necessary.

A somewhat informal committee was put together with a few men who knew the West and were willing to learn about Hollywood. Moab locals were quickly recruited. Cap Maxwell, a prominent rancher, was drafted to handle the horses and transportation. Johnnie Johnson, a farmer with great interest in the film industry, agreed to be the representative for the union laborers. Stan Peck was the natural contact for all matters pertaining to feeding the crew, since he had been running one of Moab's main restaurants for a number of years. Bish Taylor served as the buffer between the film company and the government, with emphasis on access roads and land use. Permits were not required in the early days of filming, but permission and cooperation had to be obtained, and maintained. Bish had excellent rapport with the key people in those areas.

As owner of Midland Telephone, Jack Corbin was in charge of communications. George White was primarily involved with coordinating the extras, procuring equipment, scouting, and assisting production officials. Bates Wilson, Superintendent of Arches National Park (then a Monument), worked as production assistant for John Ford. This committee was the start of the world's longest ongoing film commission on record.

Moab had been a quiet, rural county seat until Tinseltown spread its stardust and its dollars across the valley. Most residents enjoyed the excitement. Some felt the economic benefit was not worth sacrificing the serenity of their small town, but it was too late for such concerns.

The town barely had time to recover from **Wagon Master** before Ford was back with John Wayne and Maureen O'Hara to film **Rio Grande** for Republic Studios. Again, most area residents were hired. Extensive set construction was required. John Brown and Marvin Clever, both local building contractors, were added to the movie committee to help coordinate local carpenters and obtain construction materials. Grand County Sheriff J.B. Skewes, along with Edgar Wilcox, a resident "Jack-of-all-trades," served as night watchmen. There was no Moab police department in those early days of filming - just the sheriff and two deputies.

Limited telephone facilities were a major drawback. Midland Telephone had only a few circuits to the outside world. With the added population of 100 crew members - all trying to call out of the area - long distance calls were frustrating, and just one of many problems the movie committee worked to resolve.

Following **Rio Grande**, months passed with no further film activity. Eager for more business, the Movie Committee took the initiative and sent representatives to Hollywood to "sell" Moab.

Fern's Cafe/Tavern and Trav-o-tel Court, center of much activity during the early years of the film industry in Moab. Courtesy of Karl Tangren.

This photo of Midland Telephone was sent to filmmakers in early preproduction packets prepared by the Moab Movie Committee. The caption told of direct lines to various cities and stated: "On-location personnel calls will be given priority."

George White and Stan and Ruth Peck flew to Los Angeles at their own expense, each taking $150. Universal Studios provided them with a car and driver, enabling them to visit other studios as well. Unfortunately, with no brochures or photographs to sell their beautiful country, results were disappointing.

Recognizing that they could no longer take business for granted, the Movie Committee organized a fund-raising campaign for promotional materials and future trips. Stan Peck and George White drew up a list of local businesses, with their own names on top, and each gave $125. Howard Shields of the Red Rock Motel, Virginia Carter of the Utah Motel, the Lumber Yard, Midland Telephone and Ralph Miller, Sr. were among the first to make donations. Others soon followed their lead. There was one remarkable day when George and Mary Esther White (his second wife) collected $3,500.

In all, George White made ten promotional trips to the coast, often accompanied by Mary Esther. Four of these he paid for himself; on the other trips, only his traveling expenses were covered. Over the years, hundreds of Moab citizens have contributed time and money to promote the film industry in Utah's canyon country. Without this support, Moab may not have become the major film center it is today.

ECONOMIC CHANGE IN SOUTHEASTERN UTAH

In 1952, Moab prospector Charlie Steen discovered a major deposit of uranium, a rare mineral necessary to the federal government in the development of the atom bomb. Almost overnight the town's population grew from 1200 to nearly 6000. The uranium boom did not help the movie business in southeastern Utah. Moab was flooded with hopeful prospectors, the press, and curious spectators. This left little room for film crews. Not to be discouraged, the movie committee fielded complaints and continued its promotional efforts. Eventually, more motels and restaurants were built and the problem was somewhat alleviated.

*Rock Hudson with Indian boy, during filming of **Taza, Son of Cochise.** Courtesy of the Academy of Motion Picture Arts and Sciences.*

The Moab Movie Committee lured three films to Moab in 1953, **Border River; Taza, Son of Cochise;** and **Siege at Red River.** Locally hired people from Moab to Monument Valley commuted to work on films wherever they were being shot.

John Ford returned to Monument Valley in 1956 to produce **The Searchers.** This was the only movie made there during the 1950s. The Gouldings were busy with tourism and further development of their lodge and facilities. The uranium boom had impacted both San Juan County (which encompasses part of Monument Valley) and Moab by providing the Navajos and neighboring Utes with mining jobs. An expanding tourist market brought additional revenue from the sale of Native American crafts. The film industry was no longer actively pursued by the Gouldings. The Moab Movie Committee, however, often took location scouts into Monument Valley, and later expanded its boundaries to include that area.

George White continued his active role in the industry. In addition to heading up the movie committee, he often did stuntwork and was required to join the Screen Actor's Guild (for the hefty sum of $1,250) in order to work "on camera." Actors were not allowed to speak or "double" without the Guild card, and George did both in several films.

All in all, the fifties were good to Moab. Not only did the uranium industry soar, but there was an average of one film per year during the decade. Unfortunately, the economic security created by the mining boom weakened the enthusiasm for the film industry, to some extent. The unemployment rate in Grand County was low and per capita income became one of the highest in the state. The prevailing attitude was, "Why work so hard to develop the film industry when things are so comfortable?" In those days, citizens had no comprehension of the economic devastation awaiting them in the 1980s.

George White, center, talking with actors John Beal (Major John Wesley Powell, on right), and L.Q. Jones, (left) in scene from 1959 movie **Ten Who Dared**. Courtesy of George White.

Main Street Moab in early days of filming. This photo was included in promotion packages used to lure the film industry to southeastern Utah. Club 66 and the Holiday Theater were popular hangouts for film crews in the fifties and sixties.

Moab, Utah has served as a base for film companies on location in southeastern Utah since 1949. The city is situated in a beautiful valley between towering red cliffs, with the La Sal Mountains to the east. Photo taken from Poison Spider Mesa by Dan Mick.

BREAKUP OF THE STUDIO SYSTEM

Hollywood moguls were in firm control at the beginning of the fifties but, by December 1959, only Jack Warner of Warner Brothers remained. During the breakup of the studio system, production officials decided it would be more cost effective to hire their talent by the picture rather than through an annual contract. Once this occurred, stars began demanding twice as much per film, plus a percentage of the profits. As a larger portion of production budgets went to the stars, and eventually the directors, money available for location shooting diminished considerably.

By the end of the fifties the glamour of old-style Hollywood was fast becoming history. Elaborate gowns and elegant furs were replaced by T-shirts and faded blue jeans. The transition was painful, not only to the studios and some of their stars, but also to the public. Although viewers and fans loved television, Tinseltown and the cinema had always provided a larger-scope fantasy world to which the public could escape. Nostalgia is a double-edged sword, conjuring up both pleasure and sadness over things gone by. For Hollywood and its fans, a remarkable era had ended.

A NEW ERA BEGINS

As Moab entered the sixties, the movie committee began feeling the ripples of the Hollywood crisis. To increase their competitive edge for what few movies were still being filmed on location, the committee worked harder than ever to raise funds for more promotion.

New members of the Moab Movie Committee included K.E. "Ken" McDougald, then mayor of Moab and an enthusiastic advocate of the film industry, and Manuel "Bud" Lincoln, head of Grand County Employment Security. Bud had helped to supply both crew and extras for several productions. He and his wife, Jane, also ran the Prospector Lodge, popular quarters for the top stars and production officials of the day.

*Assisted by actors Roger Moore and Chill Wills, Mayor Ken McDougald cuts ribbon at opening of Moab Bowling Lanes, during time of filming **Gold of the Seven Saints**. Courtesy of The Times-Independent.*

Eight major features were produced in Moab during the sixties. Just as important, television, the "film industry stepchild," was beginning to recognize the potential of southeastern Utah landscapes. Little by little, independent film companies and ad agencies crept onto the scene, many of them interested in producing commercials or documentaries for television. In response, the movie committee restructured its strategy, beginning with a name change to the "Film" Committee. Members felt the new name would encompass television as well as the cinema.

Bud Lincoln and George White teamed up to become the core of the Moab Film Committee. Until 1985, the two men served as co-chairmen, or alternated as chairman, except for two terms when Norman Boyd, a local barber and brother-in-law to "Uranium King" Charlie Steen, and Winford Bunce, an accountant and Moab mayor, headed the group.

New promotional material was prepared, featuring forty 8x10 color photographs of beautiful canyon country, as well as illustrated scenic maps showing the Moab area. At that time, there was no Canyonlands National Park, Arches was still a national monument, and this scenic region was just beginning to be discovered by the traveling public.

George Stevens' 1963 production, *The Greatest Story Ever Told*, was the first major non-Western picture to film scenes near Moab. Other segments were shot in San Juan County and near Lake Powell. Monument Valley was the first (regionally) to become a galactic location, when part of the movie *2001: A Space Odyssey* was filmed there in 1968.

The most prominent Moab Westerns of the decade included two 20th Century Fox pictures, *The Comancheros* and *Rio Conchos*, and Warner Brothers *Cheyenne Autumn*. Part of the latter movie was also filmed in Monument Valley, as were *Sergeant Rutledge, How the West Was Won*, and *McKenna's Gold*.

In Moab, Paramount Pictures added a unique twist to the filming of the Western *Blue* in 1967. A second feature, *Fade In,* was shot at the same time. Starring Burt Reynolds, *Fade In* was the story of the filming of *Blue*. In this contemporary film, Reynolds played a Moab rancher who fell in love with the film editor of *Blue*. The official premiere of *Blue* was held in Salt Lake City. Utah Governor Cal Rampton joined the stars and the Moab Film Committee for the gala event, which included a dinner-dance at the University of Utah.

Jane and Bud Lincoln join star Ricardo Montalban and Utah Governor Cal Rampton at 1967 premiere dinner for the movie **Blue** *in Salt Lake City. Courtesy of The Times-Independent.*

TURMOIL OF THE SEVENTIES

As the sixties went over the horizon, the big Westerns faded into the sunset. With them went our classic American heroes, along with some of the patriotism of our forefathers. It seemed that defending one's country was no longer the "in" thing.

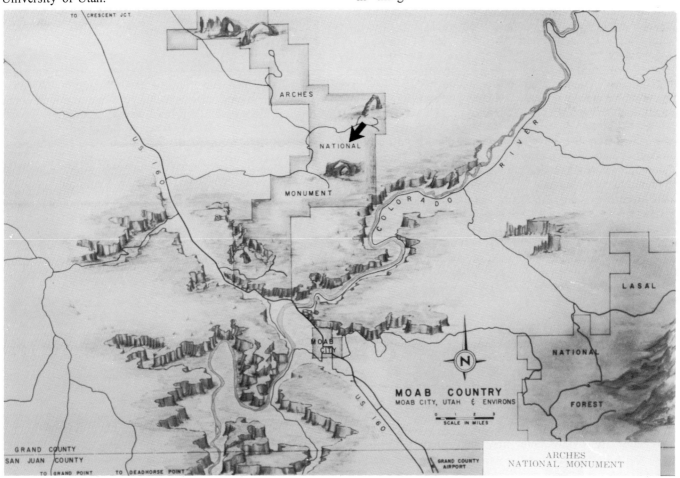

Sample of illustrated map produced in color to show film locations and proximity to Moab.

With the seventies came the burning of the American flag and peace marches. The controversial Vietnam War had run its course, and America was in a state of turmoil. These were to be the least successful years for the film industry in Moab and Monument Valley.

Although the Moab Film Committee continued promotional trips to Hollywood well into the seventies, the trips became less and less effective. The industry had changed so radically that it became difficult to identify and contact the decision-makers. The new breed of independent filmmakers were located everywhere, in every state and around the world. As a result, movies had smaller budgets and most were filmed within the confines of covered sets and sound stages. Stories requiring the great outdoors were considered too costly, especially if it meant leaving California. With sheer determination not to let its efforts falter, the film committee again restructured, this time calling itself Moab Film Development (MFD), as in "economic development."

Dixie Barker (now Barksdale), director of Grand County Community and Economic Development at the time, helped publish MFD'S first promotional brochure. MFD began to use the mail for film promotion, rather than personal contact.

In 1975, the Utah State Legislature appropriated funds for a state film development office. A director was appointed and, as the state effort took hold, it provided an excellent source of client leads.

Of six major films produced in Moab during the seventies, Universal Studios "Alias Smith and Jones" movie for television, and the Doty Dayton production of *Against A Crooked Sky,* were the most significant. The production of TV commercials, documentaries, and other television specials continued the flow of film dollars into local tills. Interest shown by still photographers mounted. Ads for magazines and billboards contributed not only to the economy but added to the exposure southeastern Utah received through the film industry.

In Monument Valley, film activity increased during the Seventies, with production of portions of *The Trial of Billy Jack*, *The Eiger Sanction*, *The Villain*, and others. Scenes from *Wild Rovers* were shot near Moab and in Monument Valley. It was also in this decade that the Gouldings sold their interests in Monument Valley and retired to southern Arizona.

COLLAPSE OF THE ECONOMY AND CHANGES FOR MOAB FILM DEVELOPMENT

With the 1980s came a decade of hard times in southeastern Utah. The economic base, which was heavily dependent upon mineral resources, was ravaged when the bottom dropped out of the mining industry in 1983. With the deterioration of the uranium business, the community rallied to chart a new direction. At a town hall meeting, scenery and the environment were identified as two of the region's most valuable assets. The film industry was maintained as a top priority, along with tourism, recreation, retirement, and compatible light industries. Economic diversity was the overriding goal for the future.

Regional competition for films was increasing as new promotion groups formed all over the country. Until this time, MFD had pretty much operated out of the hip pockets of the promoters. The only exceptions were during the sixties when the group merged with the Chamber of Commerce, which provided a part-time office, and briefly in the seventies when Dixie Barker gave assistance through the county economic and community development office. In 1982-83, Grand County Travel Council, under the direction of Marian Eason, helped MFD with telephone service, paperwork, and promotional mail-outs.

If Moab was to hold on to its film industry, it needed to upgrade its efforts. In 1984, new MFD members were recruited and the first board of directors was formed. The organization drafted bylaws and changed its name to Moab Film Promotion (MFP), believing "film development" sounded as if it belonged with a photography shop.

With the restructuring, representatives from law enforcement and public land agencies were added as resource members. Land use permits had become necessary for filming on public lands, and it was important to maintain coordination with local managers. In addition, ad-hoc committees were set up to handle specific categories of concern, such as location scouting, marketing, support resources, and a film library.

One of MFP's first tasks was to develop a new brochure. A volunteer committee, known as Moab Area Promotion (MAP), designed a beautiful 16-page, four-color booklet, which would allow each organization to insert its individual printed material. The city, county, and travel council pitched in to finance the color section of the brochure. Each organization then purchased copies at cost and printed its own black-and-white inserts. MFP's price for the total package was nominal. This document is still in use, with occasional updating of inserts.

Soon after the MFP Board was formed, a State Community Development Block Grant was awarded Grand County for a central service office and briefing center. The goal of the program was to research and prepare a five-year economic recovery plan for Grand County, while providing a full-time office and staff to serve the local economic development organizations, including film promotion. The author of this book prepared the grant application and became Executive Director.

The eighties brought more union activity nationwide. As union demands increased, production companies began to hit the road in search of lower-cost conditions for their projects. States with right-to-work laws became popular destinations for filming. Utah had become one of these states, and Moab and Monument Valley were back in business.

With Moab's revitalized organization and new capabilities, the local film industry began improving. In 1985, George White and Bud Lincoln received "Citizen of the Year" awards from the Moab Chamber of Commerce for their outstanding work in developing the local film industry.

Backlighting is used in Marlboro commercial. Southeast Utah has received world-wide exposure as "Marlboro Country."

George White and Manuel "Bud" Lincoln receiving "Citizen of the Year" awards from 1985 Chamber of Commerce President Dee Tranter. Courtesy of The Times-Independent.

Ken Sleight, long-time southern Utah tour operator, was elected president of the MFP Board of Directors in 1985, and George White was pronounced "Honorary President" for life. Ken's thrust of energy was directed at establishing a film promotion budget better reflecting its contribution to the local economy.

With the decentralization of Hollywood and the arrival of the jet age, most aspects of the film industry seemed to take on a faster pace. All responses to inquiries required express mail response. Information packets included location photo presentations to meet script requirements, as well as area promotion material and resources for production planning. Catalogues of local talent were compiled so film officials could preview the people, goods, and services available in southeastern Utah.

Sheri Griffith, who operates a river expedition company in Moab, was elected MFP president in 1986. Sheri continued Sleight's work on establishing an adequate budget to further develop the film industry. Elected for three consecutive years as president, Sheri is credited with giving real meaning to the "special committees" and "resource members" as important contributors to the effort. Community participation and enthusiasm continued to increase under her administration.

During this period Jimmie Walker, then chairman of the Grand County Commission, was a serious advocate of the film industry. Walker provided invaluable support during MFP's continued development.

Staying with its historic pattern, the organization was destined for another name change. This time it was created by a new buzz word in the industry itself: "commission." The new name was "Moab Film Commission" (MFC). Even after MFC later expanded its boundaries to include other counties, "Moab" remained in the title because of the name recognition earned over the years.

Tragedy struck the Utah film scene during the eighties. First, Harry Goulding died in 1981. This was followed by the sudden death of State Film Director John Earle, who was replaced by Leigh von der Esch. A loss hitting closer to home occurred in January of 1988 with the passing of Manuel "Bud" Lincoln.

As Grand County continued its long range economic development plan, facilities to better accommodate the film industry emerged as potential development priorities. Producers and directors filming in southeastern Utah expressed the need for a covered set or sound stage. This type of facility would allow them to film longer in the area. The Old Spanish Trail Arena was constructed by Grand County with a "covered set" in mind, as one of the facility's multiple uses.

Westerns were trying to make a comeback, and a good percentage of the scripts under consideration required an Old West town. Such a set could also be used as a theme park to attract tourism between productions. The famous Old Tucson in Arizona eventually made more money as a theme park than as a backlot for movies. The film commission continues searching for ways and means to establish a permanent Western town in Moab.

Grand County's plan also pegged museum development as relevant to increasing tourism in southeastern Utah. A Moab Movie History Museum was added to MFC's project list.

In 1986, it was brought to the attention of MFC that the "Hollywood Stuntmen's Hall of Fame" was searching for a new home. Since it would be considerable time before enough memorabilia could be collected to justify a local movie history museum, MFC pursued recruitment of the Hall of Fame. Application was made for a Utah Permanent Community Impact Board (CIB) grant, which was awarded to Moab City for the purchase of a facility to house the attraction in Moab. The grand opening of the museum was held in June 1988. A special section was dedicated to movies filmed in Moab.

Keeping up with new technology, MFC produced a

promotional video, "The Filmmaker's Perfect Location." Numbers were placed in the corner of each scene to correspond with an accompanying document, which included maps and information on miles from Moab to the location, type of roads, and permits required. The package, designed to assist producers with pre-production planning, was well received.

MFC also began documenting its film history, with major help from Carlo Gaberscek of Udine, Italy. Gaberscek spent 13 years researching for his book on classic American Western movies. He visited Moab on 12 of his trips, working like a film archaeologist. Upon examining a location site, he determines exactly where the camera was located and how the scene was played out. Many of the photos in MFC's library and museum are contributions from Gaberscek's collection.

Carlo Gaberscek and George White, during one of Gaberscek's research trips to the U.S.

MFC EXPANDS BOUNDARIES

In 1988, MFC decided to include all of San Juan County in its location promotion. By 1989, an MFC committee was formed in San Juan County, headed by Peggy Humphreys. Bret Palmer, Don Rogers, Larry Wells, Chuck Burand and Rusty Musselman assisted with locations, props and resources. Efforts were also being make to include Emery and Carbon counties.

When the Moab Film Commission joined the Association of Film Commissioners International (AFCI) in 1989, it was discovered that MFC was the longest ongoing film promotion and assistance group on record. Most commissions were only three-to-five years old at that time. It was camaraderie and enthusiasm that fueled this local film promotion organization and gave it the staying power to earn such special status.

Major productions during the eighties included nine feature pictures, part of the premiere episode of a television series, numerous TV specials, commercials, travelogues, and documentaries. Music videos were also added, as the group Heaven performed "Knockin' on Heaven's Door" on top of the Priest and the Nuns butte.

Movies filmed during this period were primarily contemporary, using Moab and Thompson as small-town America. In 1988, Vestron was filming *Sundown: Vampires in Retreat* at the same time LUCASfilms arrived to shoot the opening scenes for *Indiana Jones and the Last Crusade*. This was the first such occurrence since 1967, when *Blue* and *Fade In* were filmed simultaneously.

Other 1980s productions in Moab included *Spacehunter: Adventures in the Forbidden Zone*, *Choke Canyon*, *The Survivalist* and *Nightmare at Noon*. *The Survivalist* and *Sundown* were held "in the can," until released on video in 1992. Scenes from *The Legend of the Lone Ranger* and *National Lampoon's Vacation* were shot in Monument Valley. Eighties television series filmed in the area were "**Airwolf**" (Monument Valley) and "**MacGyver**" (Dead Horse Point State Park).

Larry Campbell was elected MFC president in 1989, bringing the fourth decade to a close. Larry, who deals mainly in real estate investment, has a side interest in vehicle fabrication, a talent soon recognized by the film industry. He had also worked in other areas of film production and brought with him front-line experience. As president, Campbell was given the dual tasks of continuing development of the film industry and implementing MFC's 40th anniversary events, which included the Moab Movie Jubliee.

*Cocktail party prior to premiere of **Nightmare at Noon**. Event was held the week of Halloween, 1988, and some film commissioners were in costume. Clowning around at the hors d'oeuvre table are Murine Ellis Gray, Karl and Loraine Tangren, Robbie Swasey, and Verle Green.*

*Local bit players in movie **Nightmare at Noon**: Nik Hougen, Larry Campbell, and Police Chief Alan West, with Vicki Herr of the Utah Film Commission.*

Moab Movie Jubilee - MFC's 40th Anniversary

*The Moab Movie Jubilee was held on Labor Day Weekend, 1989. Stars who helped MFC celebrate were John Agar (**Fort Apache**, 1948), Virginia Mayo (**Fort Dobbs**, 1956), Marie Windsor (**Alias Smith and Jones**, 1972), Don Shanks (**Grizzly Adams**, 1970s), and Moab's Vanessa Pierson (**Sundown**, 1988).*

A week after the Moab Movie Jubilee, Mike Goulding christened the new Goulding's Trading Post Museum, which includes a special section on movies made in Monument Valley. (After her husband's death, Mike had moved back to the land they so enjoyed together.)

Mike Goulding and the author browsing through old movie photos during 1989 interview. Photo by Jean Akens.

MFC published its first annual newsletter, "The Reel Report," in 1989. The report gives an accounting of MFC finances, area film activity, and the economic impact of the film industry on southeastern Utah. In addition to being an effective promotional piece, the "Reel Report" is used to say thanks to local supporters, and is enjoyed by movie buffs traveling through town.

While Grand County provided staff and an office for MFC, the board of directors was responsible for raising promotional and marketing funds. Karl Tangren, board member and public relations officer, took on the responsibility of generating nearly all necessary marketing money

Karl Tangren, 1992 recipient of MFC's coveted Special Achievement Award.

through local business contributions, plus establishing community good will. He picked up where George White and Bud Lincoln left off, on the annual fund raising effort.

An auto tour guide was developed for tourists wishing to visit various locations near Moab where movies had been filmed. Mary von Koch, MFC's resource representative from the Bureau of Land Management, compiled the information for the pamphlet, with help from Rock Smith, Superintendent of Dead Horse Point State Park. The Grand County Travel Council contributed funds for publication.

In 1989, as a member of the Association of Film Commissioners International (AFCI), MFC began its involvement with Location Expo, held each year in Los Angeles. Expo is a trade show for film commissions wishing to sell their scenery. Participants at Expo include scouts, producers, writers, and directors searching for locations to meet script requirements in upcoming productions. Contributions from the Utah Film Commission and the Grand County Travel Council have allowed MFC to participate annually in this most valuable marketing experience.

THE NINETIES AND A LOOK TO THE FUTURE

Robbie Swasey became MFC president in 1990. A member of the board since 1988, Swasey chaired the committee for the Moab Movie Jubilee. She had excellent organizational skills and served as president for two consecutive terms. During this time, MFC received a special award from the Grand County Travel Council for outstanding area promotion.

Each year more film commissions are formed to go after the "Hollywood dollars." Under Leigh van der Esch's able leadership as Utah Film Commissioner, the economic impact of the film industry in Utah continues to grow. Von der Esch served as president of the AFCI from 1991 to 1996, giving the film industry in Utah a major boost by association. When she took office, MFC was the only local or regional film commission in the state. Now included are the Southwest Utah Film Commission in St. George, Park City Film Commission, the reactivated Kanab/Kane County Film Commission, Central Utah Film Commission, Carbon/Emery Film Commission, and numerous film liaison people throughout the state. Despite this growth, the Moab Film Commission held its own.

Jim Sarten, North American River Expeditions, shows Utah Film Commissioner Leigh von der Esch (left) and MFC president Sheri Griffith locations on the Colorado River.

Carbon and Emery counties became part of MFC in 1990, with Kathy Axelgard serving as film liaison. By 1991, these two counties formed their own commission.

To the delight of most residents from Moab to Monument Valley, Westerns galloped back into the spotlight. Local rancher Don Holyoak, who had been involved with the film industry since childhood, was elected MFC president in 1992, 1993 and 1994. His background and expertise with livestock and wrangling proved especially beneficial with the returned popularity of Westerns.

Representatives from Carbon, Emery and Grand counties in MFC workshop on location scouting and photography.

During the first four years of the nineties, 23 movies were filmed in southeastern Utah, some for the theater and others for television or video. Those that have been shot mostly or entirely in the area included: **Thelma and Louise, Knights, Geronimo: An American Legend, Portals, The Jeeping Tour Adventure, Tread,** and **City Slickers II: The Search For Curly's Gold.** Features that have had segments filmed in Grand or San Juan Counties were: **Wind, Equinox, This Boy's Life, Josh and S.A.M., Double Jeopardy, Slaughter of the Innocents** (TV), **California Dreaming,** a French rock climbing movie (title unknown), **Lightning Jack, Raven Hawk, Tall Tales, The Ride, Forrest Gump** and **Pontiac Moon.** MFC also helped recruit **Rubin and Ed** and **Dark Blood** to film several scenes at nearby Wayne County's Factory Butte area. Bon Jovi and Clint Black selected southeastern Utah for music video locations.

By the 1990s the national environmental movement began to impact the film industry. Along with all other industries that utilize public lands, such as livestock grazing, mining, timber, and recreation, the film industry is being forced to change some of its traditional ways of doing business. Of the various commercial land uses, film has the shortest term use (average one-three days per location), with little impact. Most film people place high value on the special locations they select for their projects. They like to know the land will be just as beautiful when they return to film.

State and federal policy for film permitting (and enforcement), has grown much more stringent over the years. Assessments must be made by government resource specialists prior to permitting, to assure that no damage will come to wildlife, endangered plants, archaeological sites, recreational areas, and designated wilderness or wilderness study areas (WSA's). Film companies pay for these assessments, and a number of archaeological sites have been discovered through this process that may have otherwise gone undetected.

MFC joined the AFCI in its implementation of a program called "Going Green on Location." This program emphasizes care of the environment, when using nature as a stage. Film crews are reminded to stick to established trails and refrain from dropping *any* trash on the ground. Above all, when a production company is through filming, it is responsible for reclaiming the land to its "natural state," or better. There are few production sites in southeastern Utah where a visiting

19

movie buff can detect that a movie was ever filmed.

In February of 1993, the Bureau of Land Management began enforcing a 45-day permit policy (15 days for processing and 30 days for public comment) that first came to light during a Film Summit in Moab. This greatly affects the film industry in Grand and San Juan counties, where about 63 percent of the land is governed by the BLM. As a result of the policy enforcement, MFC lost about 80 percent of its television commercial and still photography work in 1993, since most such projects take less than 45 days from inception to completion.

A major campaign was initiated by MFC and the Utah Film Commission to get the permitting regulations revised and approved by the BLM. Other western-state film commissions and film associations also joined in the effort.

In June-July of 1993, several Utah congressional delegates, along with BLM's new national director, James Baca, made trips to Moab to visit the Columbia Studios set during filming of the movie **Geronimo**. They also examined other locations where reclamation had taken place in recent years. Baca formed a task force to address the policy regulating film projects that have little or no impact, primarily commercials and still photography.

Despite enforcement of the permitting process, 1993 saw 11 movies produced in the Moab area, and the economic impact continued to grow. While the more stringent policy has been troublesome for the production companies, movie schedules have more planning time up front. The newly enforced requirements do play havoc with the director's creative license, however. Should he or she decide to film someone coming into the camera from a different direction than that selected by the location manager, it might well require starting over with a new permit and 45-day processing period.

In December 1993, a new BLM policy was issued as a result of Baca's task force. It defines "minimal impact" and provides a 10-day express procedure for qualifying productions. The revised policy, however, addresses the controversial proposed HR 1500 wilderness bill as though it has already been approved by Congress, and increases requirements for film companies wishing to shoot in *proposed* wilderness areas. This means that a company wishing to film on HR 1500 land may be required to wait 75 days for a permit.

To compound the problem, all locations in Utah must be identified and listed on a single permit application before it can be processed. This allows BLM to evaluate "cumulative impact." There are often a dozen or more sites for a single movie, taking from three to six months to find. Another 75 days could kill movie making in rural Utah and other western states where wilderness is proposed.

Despite current problems, citizen support and cooperation has remained high. Without it, there would be no film industry in southeastern Utah. Each time a major feature "wraps" and goes home, the town must recover from a serious case of burnout. The fast pace of film production and the demands it puts on a community are exhausting. But as time has proven, from Moab to Monument Valley, residents have plenty of gusto and maintain a vision of better things to come.

In 1993, the changing political climate forced MFC to rethink its quasi-government status. The Moab-Monument Valley Arts and Film Association was formed, as a nonprofit corporation to solicit funds for the film commission and its

museum and library. Other related arts and film projects will be considered for funding in the future, once existing programs are stabilized.

Also in 1993, MFC changed its name once more, and "Moab to Monument Valley Film Commission" (MMVFC) became the new title. The change was made to increase name recognition, since Monument Valley is known worldwide, and because it more accurately defines the boundaries of the film commission. It is anticipated that making the film commission independent from government will take several years of intensive fundraising.

Association of Film Commissioners International (AFCI) Location Expo, held each year in Los Angeles, California.

The author, Peggy Humphreys (representing San Juan County), and MFC President Robbie Swasey in booth at Expo. Photo by Nancy Valmer.

Utah Governor and Mrs. Bangeter visit with Native American dancers from Blanding at "Evening in John Ford Country," sponsored by MFC.

Ms. Peng Xiaolian, film director from the People's Republic of China, on Canyonlands National Park tour arranged through Visitor Program Service International, Washington, D.C. A visitor with the U.S. Exchange Program, Peng was hosted by Bob Jones, Tag-A-Long Expeditions, and the author.

MFC float, with Western theme, in one of the many parades held in Moab throughout the year.

Brad and Laura Fulton, Salt Lake City, visit the Moab-Monument Valley Film Museum and Library, at the MFC office in Moab.

THE DIGITAL REVOLUTION

The greatest changes ever to hit the film industry are predicted for the 1990s. There are some who believe that computer digital imaging will eventually eliminate the need for location filming. Steven D. Katz, in his article "The Digital Backlot" (Millimeter Magazine, March 1993) comments: "The sharks, Kongs, and stunt shows of the Universal Studio Tour may be all that's left of traditional stagecraft, as megabytes of computer code become the stuff dreams are made of."

Katz notes that Greg Panos, publisher of "Virtual Reality Sourcebook," is offering his service through Personaform (a system he developed) as a way of preserving our idealized selves for future generations. Through Personaform, a completely convincing animated 3-D model is created that can interact with living persons. It would appear that movie stars are also vulnerable to this new technology and could become an endangered species.

Film commissioners everywhere are challenged with how to adapt to this new age of technology. The Moab to Monument Valley Film Commission is scrambling to do the same.

It is predicted that there will be about 500 new cable television channels that will be used for a multitude of things. Books will be replaced by computer disks, in the home and classroom. There will still be a need for some location filming, but only for short periods of time, with two to four crew people. For a while, at least, there will still be producers who want the real thing. As digital imaging is perfected and becomes less expensive, it may be only big-budget movie producers who seek out actual locations. Even then, computer technology will likely be combined to create the final product.

The new thrust by film commissioners will be to attract to their respective areas the high-tech companies that will be introducing the new film concept to the world. Since most such communication systems do not require big city settings, the Moab-to-Monument Valley area has a lot to offer. The quality of life found in such a pristine corner of the world can be very enticing. The artistic, intelligent people who run the computer digital systems will need to occasionally escape their machines, and there is nothing like a jaunt through magnificent canyon country to inspire and rejuvenate the human species.

High-tech changes are expected to generate new interest in film history. The Moab-Monument Valley Film Museum and Library, located at Red Cliff Adventure Lodge (14 miles up Scenic Highway 128), will be working to acquire and preserve more memorabilia pertaining to projects filmed in Utah.

* * *

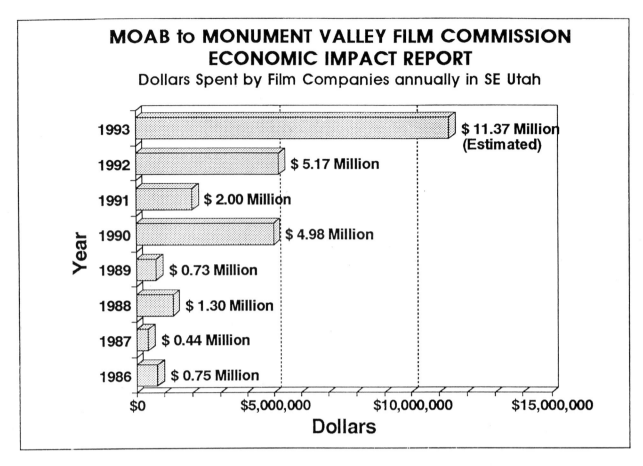

MOAB to MONUMENT VALLEY FILM COMMISSION
ECONOMIC IMPACT REPORT
Dollars Spent by Film Companies annually in SE Utah

Year

- 1993 — $ 11.37 Million (Estimated)
- 1992 — $ 5.17 Million
- 1991 — $ 2.00 Million
- 1990 — $ 4.98 Million
- 1989 — $ 0.73 Million
- 1988 — $ 1.30 Million
- 1987 — $ 0.44 Million
- 1986 — $ 0.75 Million

$0 $5,000,000 $10,000,000 $15,000,000

Dollars

The money reported as left in southeastern Utah by film companies is the actual dollars that MMVFC staff has been able to trace. Film crews also invest in recreational tours and various gifts that are not traceable. The economic impact as shown in the chart above is therefore less than the amount actually spent in the area.

George White, founder of the Moab Film Commission, with Life Time Achievement Award presented in 1993.

*MMVFC designs memorabilia T-shirts for the movies filmed in the area, which are then sold to raise funds for marketing southeastern Utah. Film commissioner Robbie Swasey and assistant director Kari Murphy display **Thelma and Louise** shirts.*

MOAB TO MONUMENT VALLEY FILM COMMISSION

BOARD OF DIRECTORS - 1984-2000

George White 1984 – HONRARY PRESIDENT
FOR LIFE
Manuel "Bud" Lincoln – 1984-1986
David White – 1984-1986
Dennis Sweeney – 1984-1986
Ken Sleight – 1984-1985
Bette Stanton – 1984
Dennis Lesmeister – 1984
Mitch Williams – 1984
Larry Campbell – 1985-1996
J. J. Wang – 1985-1988
Steve Kennedy – 1985
Sheri Griffith – 1985-1991
Don Holyoak – 1985-2000
Karl Tangren – 1987-1996 & 1999-2000
Scott Cockayne – 1987
Ber Knight – 1987-1989
Jackie Johnson – 1988-1991
Antony Landsman – 1988-1989
Jim Mattingly – 1988-1991
Jim Kelly – 1988-1991
Roland Bringhurst – 1988
Robbie Swasey – 1989-1992
Renee Wallis – 1989
Bonnie Lindgren – 1989-1994 & 1995-1996
Kurt Balling – 1990-1991
Verle Green – 1990-1992
Brett Palmer (San Juan County) – 1990
Larris Hunting (Emery County) – 1991
Michelle Donohue (Carbon County) – 1991
Jean Akens – 1991-1996
Ron Griffith – 1992-1994
Bego Gerhart – 1992-1995
Hugh Glass – 1992-1994
Richard Farabee – 1992-1994
Joe Kiffmeyer – 1994-1995
Lorri Morgan – 1995-2000
Theresa Eggeling – 1995-2000
Carl Anderson – 1995-1997
Jimmy Walker – 1995-1999
Jennie Massie – 1995-2000
Montez Steele – 1996-2000
Dave Fincham – 1997-2000
Reggie Blatter – 1997-1999
Cliff Eggeling – 1997-2000
Don Swartz – 1997-1998
Wylie Gerrard – 1999-2000
James Ferro – 2000

SAN JUAN COUNTY SATELLITE COMMITTEE

Chuck Burand	Larry Wells
Rusty Musselman	Don Rogers
Bill Thompson	Fred Cly

Over the years, ex-officio members were appointed to the Board from Moab City and the counties that contributed financially to the effort.

FILM COMMISSION RESOURCE MEMBERS

Mary von Koch – BLM – (Grand County)
David Krouskop – BLM – (San Juan County)
Gordon Topham – Dead Horse Point State Park
Rock Smith – Dead Horse Point State Park
Eugene Swalberg – Dead Horse Point State Park
Nick Eason – National Park Service
Larry Thomas – National Park Service
Pat Spahr – United States Forest Service
Bob Jones – Travel Council
Doug Squires – Grand County Sheriff's Department
Tony Schetzsle – Canyonlands National Park
John McLaughlin – Arches National Park
Jim Webster – Arches National Park
Paul Cowan – Arches National Park
Clayton Allred – Utah Highway Patrol
Sandra Holloway – Canyonlands National Park
Jan Parmenter – State Lands
Mike Navarre, Scott Mallon, Alan West – City Police
Barbara Ekker – Wayne County liaison
Eugene Swalberg – Goblin Valley State Park
Dave Hutchinson – Grand County Roads & Highways

FILM COMMISSION STAFF

Betty Jacobs (part time under Chamber) - 1967
Marian Eason (part time under Travel Council) - 1984
Bette L. Stanton, Executive Director – 1984-1996
Sandi Larna – 1984-1985
Dina McCandless – 1985-1986
Charlene Ritter – 1986-1987
Tina Lopez – 1986-1994
Tammy Snow – 1992-1994
Kathy Alelgard – (Carbon/Emery counties) - 1990
Peggy Humphreys – (San Juan County) – 1989-2004
Karie Murphy – 1986-1996 when she became
Executive Director – 1996-2001
Ken Davey, Executive Director – 2001 to present

OTHER COMMISSION MEMBERS

Cheryl East	Joseph Braley
Sharon Sidwell	Tim Higgs
George Chritton	B. J. Griffith
Fred Lazarus	Shannon Lavender Rowe
Renee LaFaurie	Aaron Lavery
Becky Knouff	Murine Ellis
Diane Nelson	Yvonne Pierson
Dale Pierson	Ray Tibbetts
Myke Hughes	Monte Bowthorpe
Connie Shaeffer	Mary Engleman
Janet Dutilly	Leo Dutilly
Larry Walker	Jack Goodspeed
Bruce Keeler	Mike Holyoak

1984 AD-HOC COMMITTEES: Bob Jones (marketing), Lyle Jamison (location scouting) Steve Kennedy (recreation), M. L. Terry (communications), and Sam Taylor (brochure).

Grand County dissolved the board in 2001 when it moved MMVFC under the Travel Council.

A rainbow drops into breathtaking Monument Basin below Grand View Point, Canyonlands National Park. This unique canyon roughly resembles a giant dinosaur track.

Nokaito Bench, in tapestry colors of blue, pink and mauve, to the east of Mexican Hat, Utah, where the lazy San Juan River cuts a path around the tiny community.

HEROES AND LEADING LADIES

The stage is set, the scenery spectacular, but it's the Hollywood "stars" who inject life into a scene. Every plot must have a hero and most every hero his leading lady. Surprisingly, a review of the movies produced in Utah's rugged canyon country reveals a shortage of leading ladies. It would appear that many of the earlier films were of such a wild and wooly nature that females didn't fit into the scripts. That image changed, however, when Geena Davis and Susan Sarandon starred in *Thelma and Louise.*

Some of the best male and female leads in show business have starred in Moab-Monument Valley movies. It is to these film greats that this chapter is dedicated, along with the many actors and actresses who played support roles and character parts on location in southeastern Utah.

John Wayne, the ultimate hero, starred in: **Stagecoach** *- 1938;* **Fort Apache** *- 1949;* **She Wore a Yellow Ribbon** *- 1949, all Monument Valley;* **Rio Grande** *- 1950, Moab;* **The Searchers** *- 1956, Monument Valley;* **The Comancheros** *- 1961, and a cameo role in* **The Greatest Story Ever Told** *- 1963, Moab. Courtesy of The Academy of Motion Picture Arts and Sciences.*

*John Hodiak and Judy Garland in scene from **The Harvey Girls**, a 1946 release with segments shot in Monument Valley.*

*Victor Mature and Linda Darnell in **My Darling Clementine**, a 1946 production filmed in Monument Valley.*

*Ben Johnson and Joanne Dru, stars of Moab's first movie, **Wagon Master**, filmed in 1949. Courtesy of The Academy of Motion Picture Arts and Sciences.*

*Van Johnson and Joanne Dru, as they appear in **Siege at Red River**, on location in Moab, 1953.*

Jeffrey Hunter and Natalie Wood in scene from **The Searchers***, on set in Monument Valley, 1955.*

Clint Walker and Virginia Mayo, the leads in **Fort Dobbs***, filmed on location in Moab and Kanab, Utah, 1956.*

Jeffrey Hunter and Constance Towers in Monument Valley Western **Sergeant Rutledge***, 1960.*

Richard Widmark and Carroll Baker in **Cheyenne Autumn***, 1963, filmed in Moab and Monument Valley.*

*Terence Stamp and Joanna Pettet in movie **Blue**, shot on locations around Moab in 1967.*

*Burt Reynolds and Barbara Loden in scene from **Fade In**, filmed in 1967. This movie also starred Moab as Moab. Courtesy of The Academy of Motion Picture Arts and Sciences.*

*Bo Hopkins and Kimberly Ross starred in **Nightmare at Noon**, shot in and around Moab in 1987.*

*Bruce Boxleitner and Rachel Ward, stars of made-for-TV movie **Double Jeopardy**, filmed in part near Moab in 1992. Photo by Bego Gerhart.*

*Jeff Chandler and Rock Hudson in **Taza, Son of Cochise**, on location in Professor Valley, 1953. Courtesy of The Academy of Motion Picture Arts and Sciences.*

*Maureen O'Hara, John Wayne's leading lady, in **Rio Grande**, seen here with film son, actor Claude Jarman, Jr. O'Hara has fainted in this shot.*

*Geena Davis and Susan Sarandon in title roles of **Thelma and Louise**, filmed in Grand and San Juan counties. Photo by Larry Nagel.*

ACTORS
* Local Actors

Victor Aaron
Rodolfo Acasta
Michael Adams
John Agar
Hrant Alianak
Rex Allen
Richard Dean Anderson
Warner Anderson
Dana Andrews
Michael Ansara
Morris Ankrum
Richard Arlen
Pedro Armendariz
James Arness
Dana Ashbrook
Joe Don Baker
Stephen Baldwin
Walter Baldwin
George Bancroft
Richard Basehart
Monty Bass
John Beal
Jim Beaver
Don Beddoe
Alfonso Bedoya
Pipe Line Begishe *
Noah Beery
Michael Bell
Jean-Paul Belmondo
Burnette Bennett
Reggie Bennett
Bill Benson
Ron Berger
James Best
Exactly Sonnie Betsuie*
Chief Big Tree
Wes Bishop
Clint Black
Harry Black Horse *
Robert Blake
Ward Bond
Mark Boone, Jr.
Richard Boone
Jon Bon Jovi
Paul Boretski
Ernest Borgnine
Dan Borzage
Willis Bouchey
Rudy Bowman
Bruce Boxleitner
Christopher Bradley
Lee Bradley *
Frank Bradley *
Buff Brady
Ed Brady
Henry Brandon
Walter Brennan
Jim Brown
Roger Aaron Brown
Edgar Buchanan
Robert Burton
Bruce Cabot
Roger Callard

Jesse Cameron
Rod Cameron
Larry Campbell *
Bruce Campbell
J.D. Cannon
Yakima Canutt
Harry Carey, Jr.
David Carradine
John Carradine
Beeson Carroll
Billy Cartledge
Jack Cassidy
Maxwell Caulfield
Jeff Chandler
Robert Charlebois
Chevy Chase
Berton Churchill
Eduardo Cianneli
Steve Clemente
Lee J. Cobb
Bill Cody
Peter Coe
Stephen Collins
Russell Collins
Gary Combs
Luis Contreras
Tommy Cook
Kevin Corcoran
Anthony Costello
Bruce Cowling
Walter Coy
Buster Crabbe
Scott Crabbe
Everett Creach
Billy Crystal
Ken Curtis
Richard Cutting
George Dale
Matt Damon
Ted Danson
Michael Dante
Thayer David
Jim Davis
Roger Davis
Sam Dawson
John Day
Lee de Brouix
Joe De Santis
Cliff De Young
Vince Deadrick, Jr.
Robert De Niro
Andy Devine
Leonard Di Caprio
Richard Dix
Brian Donlevy
Tommy Doss
Kirk Douglas
Tom Drake
James Drury
Michael Dugan
Keir Dullea
Robert Duvall
Carlos East
Clint Eastwood
Buddy Ebsen
John Eckert

Richard Egan
Jack (Jones) Eiseman
Jack Elam
Bud Elkins
Stephen Elliott
Jon Epstein
Erik Estrada
Gene Evans
Richard Farnsworth
Hugh Farr
Karl Farr
Len Felber
Frank Ferguson
Jose Ferrer
Steve Ferry
John Finn
Shug Fisher
Noah Fleiss
Buck Flower
Henry Fonda
Peter Fonda
Dick Foran
Francis Ford
Harrison Ford
Wallace Ford
Preston Foster
Michael J. Fox
Tony Franciosa
Lance Fuller
Robert Fuller
M.C. Gainey
Richard Garland
Don Garner
Jerry Gatlin
Bill Gettinger
Stathis Giallelis
Scott Glenn
Crispin Glover
George Godwin
Cuba Gooding, Jr.
Greg Goossen
Marjoe Gortner
Greg Graham
Rodney A. Grant
Stuart "Proud Eagle" Grant
Michael Green
Graham Greene
Mark Gregory
Pete Grey Eyes *
Moses Gunn
Steve Guttenberg
Gene Hackman
Larry Hagerman
Anthony Michael Hall
Ben Hall
John Hall
Fred Hampton *
James Hampton
Raymond Harmstorf
Gordon Hansen
Paul Harper
Jared Harris
Feather Hat, Jr. *
Wings Hauser
Chuck Hayward
Van Heflin

Lawrence Heller
Bob Henderson
Lance Henrickson
Bill Henry
Juano Hernandez
Charlton Heston
Howard Hesseman
Harold Hickman *
Slim Hightower
Craig Hill
Terence Hill
John Hodiak
William Hoffer
Pato Hoffman
Pat Hogan
Paul Hogan
Kevin Hogen
William Holden
Tim Holt
Dennis Hopper
Bo Hopkins
Charles Horvath
Nik Hougen *
Hoke Howell
Bobby Hoy
Rock Hudson
Ernie Hudson
Jeffrey Hunter
Ray Hyke
Gene Iglesias
Miguel Inclan
Jack Ingraham
John Ireland
Michael Ironside
Brad Jackson
Dean Jagger
Mike Jajjar
Brion James
David Janssen
Claude Jarman, Jr.
Ben Johnson
LeRoy Johnson
Noble Johnson
Van Johnson
Stan Jones
Gordon Jones
Billy Jones
L.Q. Jones
Victor Jory
Cornelius Keefe
Harvey Keitel
Brian Keith
Barry Kelly
De Forest Kelley
Charles Kemper
Arthur Kennedy
Ford Kennedy
Fred Kennedy
George Kennedy
Guy Kibbee
David Klekas
Vince Klyn
Shawn Knutson *
Kris Kristofferson
Geofrey Land
Steven Lang

Theordore Larch
Walt LaRue
Tom Laughlin
Justin Lavender
Al Lee
Duke Lee
Fred Libby
Judson Keith Linn
Robert Lipton
Cleavon Little
Christopher Lloyd
Gary Lockwood
Jon Lovitz
Away Luna *
John Lund
Cliff Lyons
Ian MacDonald
William H. Macy
Michael Madsen
Karl Malden
Peter Mamokos
Jim Many Goats *
Bob Many Mules *
Art Manzanares *
Chris Pin Martin
Richard Martin, Jr.
Lee Marvin
Louis Mason
Raymond Massey
Ron Masters
Victor Mature
Michael Maxim-Nader
Mike Mazurki
Sean McClory
Joel McCrea
Christopher McDonald
J. Farrell McDonald
Lee McGloughlin
Walter McGrail
Frank McGrath
Malcolm McGregor
Stephen McHattie
Victor McLaglen
Gary McLarty
Paul McVey
Donald Meek
Ralph Meeker
Gerardo Mejia
Louis Mercier
Burgess Meredith
Jim Metzler
Robert Middleton
David H. Miller
Sal Mineo
Michael Minzares
Thomas Mitchell
Matthew Modine
Jack Mohr
Ricardo Montalban
Monty Montana
Clayton Moore
Roger Moore
Dick Moran
Doug Morck *
Antonio Moreno
Alberto Morin

Jeff Morrow
Alan Mowbray
Ben Murphy
J. Carroll Naish
Tatsuya Nakadai
Barry Newman
Jack Nicholson
Hugh O'Brian
Edmond O'Brien
George O'Brien
Jimmy O'Hara
Kent Odell
Jackie Old Coyote
Ryan O'Neal
Peter Ortiz
Carlos Palomino
Jack Palance
Gregg Palmer
Post Park
Lloyd "Sunshine" Parker
Jason Patric
Gregory Peck
Steve Pendleton
Jack Pennick
George Peppard
Joseph Perry
Lloyd Perryman
Nehemiah Persoff
House Peters, Jr.
Stewart Peterson
River Phoenix
Bill Phipps
Mitch Pileggi
Brad Pitt
Noam Pitlik
Pete Plastow *
Oliver Platt
Sidney Poitier
Judson Pratt
Nicholas Pryor
Jonathan Pryce
Denver Pyle
John Qualen
Anthony Quayle
Anthony Quinn
Steve Railsback
Claude Rains
Rex Reason
Walter Reed
Steve Reevis
Burt Reynolds
William Reynolds
Toby Richards
Clint Ritchie
Joseph Rickson
Jason Robards
Edward G. Robinson
Chuck Roberson
Roy Roberts
Bart Roberts
Walter Robles
Gilbert Roland
Buddy Roosevelt
Michael Rudd
Billy Green Rush
Bing Russell

Michael Ryan
Ron Samuels
Telly Savalas
Joe Sawyer
William Schellert
Anthony Schmidt
John Schock
Arnold Schwarzenegger
Veto Scolie
Charles Seel
Bill Shannon
Omar Sharif
Jim Shepard
Arthur Shields
Percy Shooting Star *
Jay Silverheels
Mickey Simpson
Russell Simpson
Frank Sinatra, Jr.
Tom Skerritt
Chief Sky Eagle
Sonny Skyhawk
Dean Smith
Many Mules Son *
The Sons of the Pioneers
Douglas Spencer
Klinton Spilsbury
Vincent St. Cyr
Nick Stahi
Terence Stamp
Daniel Stern
Charles Stevens
James Stewart
Milburn Stone
Peter Strauss
Woody Strode
Wes Studi
Don Summers
Bo Svenson
Patrick Swayze
Tetsuva Takida
William Talman
Karl Tangren *
Robert Taylor
Harry Tenbrook
Kevin Tighe
Reno Thunder
Jim Thorpe
Jacob Tierney
Jack Tin Horn *
Ryan Todd
Regis Toomey
Tom Tyler

Robert Urich
James Van Horn
Dale Van Sickle
Gil Van Waggoner
Mario Van Peebles
Jan-Michael Vincent
Max von Sydow
Charles Wagenheim
John Waite
Clint Walker
Rock Walker
Robert Walker
Norman Walki
Eli Wallach
Arthur Walsh
M. Emmett Walsh
Jonathan Ward
Bryant Washburn
David Wayne
John Wayne
Patrick Wayne
William Wellman, Jr.
Alan West *
James Westerfield
Dan White
George E. White *
Chief White Horse
Smile White Sheep *
Stuart Whitman
Richard Widmark
Henry Wilcoxon
John Wildman
Raleigh Wilson
Scott Wilson
Jack Williams
Fred Williamson
Jack Willis
Bob Willke
Chill Wills
Henry Wills
Raleigh Wilson
Terry Wilson *
Grant Withers
Harry Woods
Hank Worden
Al Wyatt
Ed Wynn
Keenan Wynn
Billy Yellow *
Carleton Young
J. Young
Joe Yrigoyen

Joel McCrea

ACTRESSES

* Local Actresses

Elizabeth Allen
Launa Anderson
Dorothy Appleby
Beulah Archuletta
Dana Ashbrook
Carroll Baker
Ina Balin
Ellen Barkin
Kimberly Beck
Alma Beltrand
Brenda Benus
Karen Black
Juanita Blackwater *
Susan Blakely
Jewell Blanch
Wiggie Blowne
Lara Flynn Boyle
Morgan Brittany
Fritzi Brunette
Barbara Burck
Billie Burke
Susan Cabot
Olive Carey
Lynn Carlin
Helena Carroll
Patricia Casey
Movita Castenada
Nora Cecil
Cyd Charisse
Ruth Clifford
Imogene Coca
Dorothy Conrad
Beverly D'Angelo
Carmen D'Antonio
Marga Daighton
Leora Dana

Linda Darnell
Jane Darwell
Geena Davis
Judy Davis
Yvonne De Carlo
Dolores Del Rio
Bo Derek
Catherine Destiville
Patsy Dole
Cathy Downs
Joanne Dru
Marion Eaton
Virginia Ellis
Shannon Farnon
Brenda Flower
Deborah Foreman
Judy Garland
Helen Gibson
Annie Girardot
Mary Gordon
Erin Gourlay
Elizabeth Gracen
Jennifer Grey
Sheri Griffith *
Karolyn Grimes
Jane Hampton
Moira Harris
Elayne Heilveil
Jane Hoag
Arabella Holzbog
Nancy Hsueh
Carolyn Jones
Shirley Jones
Dorothy Jordan
Janet Julian
Phyllis Kirk
Sally Kirkland
Helen Kleeb
Florence Lake

Angela Lansbury
Eva Larson
Teresa Laughlin
Piper Laurie
Anna Lee
Jacquelin Lee
Peggy Lipton
Kathy Long
Barbara Loden
Dorothy Malone
Andrea Marcovivvi
Ann-Margret
Trina Marquez
Mae Marsh
Marion Mason
Virginia Mayo
Vonetta McGee
Rachel McLigh
Victoria Medlin
Dolores Michaels
Vera Miles
Leticia Moman
Nanomba "Moonbeam"
    Morton
Mildred Natwick
Eva Novak
Catherine O'Hara
Maureen O'Hara
Kathleen O'Malley
Vesta Pegg
Joanna Pettet
Vanessa Pierson *
Louise Platt
Martha Plimpton
Deborah Pratt
Patricia Pretzinger
Victoria Racimo
Ivalou Redd *
Debbie Reynolds

Irene Rich
Molly Ringwald
Elvira Rios
Rachel Roberts
Kimberly Ross
Barbara Rush
Susan Sarandon
Pippa Scott
Aliesa Shirley
Davina Smith
Margaret Smith
Camilla Sparv
Mary Steinburgen
Jan Styne
Delores Taylor
Shirley Temple
Tetsuva Takida
Rino Thunder
Cali Timmins
Sheila Tousey
Constance Towers
Claire Trevor
Tara Trimble *
Beverly Tyler
Sara Vardi
Isela Vega
Brenda Venus
Mary Kathleen Walker
Wende Wagner
Rachel Ward
Sela Ward
Patricia Wettig
Margaret Willey
Lois Wilson
Marie Windsor
Shelley Winters
Estelle Winwood
Lana Wood
Natalie Wood

*Morgan Brittany, star of the movie **Sundown**.*

Yvonne DeCarlo. Courtesy of The Academy of Motion Picture Arts and Sciences.

THE DIRECTORS

The silver screen has always generated a special mystique. Popular conversation often buzzes with tidbits about the newest star or latest box office attraction. Publicity agents work tirelessly to show their clients in the most elegant of social circumstances. But in recent years, it is often the directors who take the spotlight. In fact, the ultimate goal of many outstanding actors is to someday become a director.

According to The Film Encyclopedia by Ephraim Katz, a director is "...the person responsible for the creative aspects, both interpretive and technical, of a motion picture production." On location he or she orchestrates the scene, actors, and equipment to produce the intended effect. It is his or her vision that comes out on film. In Hollywood, the buck stops here!

For nearly seven decades, Moab and Monument Valley have had the pleasure of hosting some of Hollywood's greatest film directors. Because of the area's role in production support, the directors have become better known locally than many of the actors. Their identities, backgrounds, and the movies they came to film in canyon country may surprise some. The foreign birth of many directors exhibits both the lure of Hollywood and the American West as a theme. From John Ford to Steven Spielberg, each director has contributed to southeastern Utah's film history. Featured here are some of the more prominent directors.

GEORGE B. SEITZ
Directed: *The Vanishing American* (1925) and *Kit Carson* (1940)

Born January 2, 1888, Seitz became involved in the arts, first as an illustrator, then as an actor and playwright. He collaborated on the script *The Perils of Pauline* and other classic Pearl White serials.

Seitz entered films in 1913 and eventually established his own studio and produced, directed, and sometimes starred in his productions. Serials were his specialty and he virtually dominated the field until 1925. His silent features were usually action-filled and often Westerns. With sound, many of his pictures took on a lighter theme, such as the Andy Hardy series.

A perfectionist, Seitz came in on schedule with his films, and on or below budget. He produced over 100 features, sometimes doing four or five a year. Some of his Westerns were *Wild Horse Mesa* (1925), *The Last Frontier* (1926), and *The Last of the Mohicans* (1936).

JOHN FORD
Directed: *Stagecoach* (1939), *My Darling Clementine* (1946), *Fort Apache* (1948), *She Wore a Yellow Ribbon* (1949), *Wagon Master* (1949), *Rio Grande* (1950), *The Searchers* (1956), *Sergeant Rutledge* (1960), and *Cheyenne Autumn* (1963)

A hero to many in southeastern Utah for the classic Westerns he filmed here, Ford was born Sean Aloysis O'Feeney in Cape Elizabeth, Maine, on February 1, 1895. In 1913 he joined his brother, Francis Ford, in Hollywood, where Francis worked as an actor, writer, and director at Universal Studios. Francis was able to get Sean, alias Jack Ford (who would not become known as John Ford until 1923), a job as set laborer and assistant propman.

Ford moved rapidly up the ladder at Universal, becoming a director by 1917. His first movie was *Straight Shooting*, which won him considerable recognition for his natural skills, including his choice of locations. Before moving to 20th Century Fox in 1920, Ford made 30 films, mostly Westerns. His reputation as one of America's great film directors, however, was not established until the 1930s and 1940s. This he accomplished through classics such as *Stagecoach*, the movie that launched John Wayne, whom Ford would eventually direct in 31 films.

John Ford was a sensitive man, with an ability to express feelings and stir emotions. He knew the heart of America and what it wanted to see on the screen. His Westerns captured the universal patterns of human experience. The conflicts portrayed in his pictures, between light and shadow, man and nature, good and evil, society and the individual, were done with such skill that viewers from all walks of life could relate to the characters and circumstances. The West was seen as clean and pure, yet rugged. It made a perfect setting for his movies.

Ford took his directing very seriously and his drive for authenticity in costume, props, and other historical elements was quite impressive. He had a special way of projecting the many dimensions of the unique southeastern Utah landscapes onto the screen. To gain perspective, he would stretch out the cavalry from the furthest point and bring them straight into the camera. On other occasions, sprinkling Indians across the scene, or having a lone rider gallop forward from a distant formation, would produce the desired effect. Ford's methods and style have long been admired by the industry and public alike.

*John Ford with star Richard Widmark, on location with **Cheyenne Autumn**. Ford is carrying his famous handkerchief that he would nervously chew when tension developed on set. Courtesy of George White.*

GEORGE SHERMAN

Directed: ***Battle at Apache Pass*** (1952) and ***Border River*** (1953) He also returned to Moab as the producer for ***The Comancheros*** in 1961

George Sherman, born on July 14, 1908, in New York City, also specialized in Westerns. A very prolific director, he put out more than 100 movies and 250 episodes of TV series. Starting as an assistant director in the early 1930s, Sherman directed his first movie, ***Wild Horse Rodeo***, in 1937. He directed many low-budget Westerns for Republic Studios, then graduated to medium-budget movies at Columbia Pictures in the mid-1940s.

By the time he discovered the filming potential of Utah, Sherman was with Universal-International. Starting in Kanab, he directed ***Black Bart***, followed by ***Red Canyon*** and ***Calamity Jane and Sam Bass***, both filmed in 1949.

As with Ford, Sherman's pictures displayed plenty of Indians and cavalry. He was also quick to take advantage of available opportunities. While filming ***Battle at Apache Pass*** near Moab, he used the fort left by Ford in ***Rio Grande***. To create a special mood, he made the most of bad weather during that picture. As the U.S. 7th Cavalry prepared to ride off to meet their demise, the sky clouded up and the wind blew billows of dust in their trail. This powerful effect was just what Sherman wanted and could never have achieved on set, without special effects.

GORDON DOUGLAS

Directed: ***Fort Dobbs*** (1956), ***Gold of the Seven Saints*** (1960), and ***Rio Conchos*** (1964)

Gordon Douglas was born on December 5, 1909. A native New Yorker, he began his stage career while still a toddler. He made it to Hollywood in the late 1920s, working as both an actor and casting director. Douglas was best known during the early years for directing "Our Gang" comedy shorts; he also co-directed the feature ***General Spanky*** in 1936. Of the many motion pictures he directed from 1939 through the 1970s, his specialty was comedy, later changing to action-adventure.

Of the three movies Douglas directed in Moab, ***Rio Conchos*** was the most action-filled. In all three movies, he utilized the Colorado River as much as the script would allow; directing action on the banks and in the water was a challenge. For these scenes, he obtained technical assistance from George White and others well-acquainted with river conditions.

34

*Director Gordon Douglas chats with actor Richard Boone while filming **Rio Conchos**, on location in Professor Valley. Courtesy of George White.*

DOUGLAS SIRK
Directed: *Taza, Son of Cochise* (1953)

Skagen, Denmark was the birthplace of Claus Detlev Kierk on April 26, 1900. Sirk studied drama in Germany while still in his teens. Changing his name to fit the country, Detlef Hans Sierck became a successful stage producer and director. In 1934, because of his leftist views following the Nazi rise to power, he changed to film, for the Nazi regime had less control over the international film market. Despite his achievements in Europe, when relocating in Hollywood during the late 1930s he was virtually unknown. German names were unpopular following World War I, so he changed his name to Douglas Sirk. The first movie he directed in the United States was **Hitler's Madmen**.

Most of Sirk's projects were low-budget, with mediocre scripts, until the 1950s. **Magnificent Obsession** was among his better movies, and was filmed the same year as *Taza, Son of Cochise*, with the same male lead, Rock Hudson. For health reasons, Sirk retired from the industry in 1959 to live in Munich, Germany.

*Director Douglas Sirk going over lines with Moab's Barbara Burck on set of **Taza, Son of Cochise**. Courtesy of Barbara Burck Cathey.*

35

EDWARD DMYTRYK
Directed: *Warlock* (1958)

Despite the ancestry of his name, Dmytryk was Canadian, born September 4, 1908. He started working at age 15 as a messenger boy for Paramount Studios in Hollywood. His directing career began in 1935. *Crossfire*, his 1947 feature, was Hollywood's first serious attempt to deal with stories involving racial discrimination. An emotionally gripping movie, it won acclaim from film critics.

In 1947, the House Un-American Activities Committee investigated and found Dmytryk guilty of Communist Party affiliations. He was sentenced to a year in jail as one of the "Hollywood Ten." Following his release, he went into a self-imposed exile in England. Returning to the United States in 1951 to provide testimony in a second round of hearings, Dmytryk helped incriminate several of his former colleagues. He was then removed from the Hollywood "blacklist" and went on to direct such credible films as *Broken Lance* and *The Caine Mutiny*.

Warlock was among the few Westerns Dmytryk directed. All exterior scenes, with the exception of the western street, were filmed on locations near Moab.

MICHAEL CURTIZ
Directed: *The Comancheros* (1961)

Born Nihaly Kertesz, December 24, 1888, in Budapest, Hungary, Curtiz entered Hungarian filmmaking in 1912. Following World War I, he sought political refuge in Germany and then in Austria. Harry Warner brought him to Hollywood in 1926, where he soon changed his name to Michael Curtiz. Over the next 25 years, he directed more than 100 films for Warner Brothers. He may best be remem-

bered for his romantic adventures starring Errol Flynn.

In the 1950s, Curtiz left Warner Brothers and was with 20th Century Fox when he filmed *The Comancheros*, starring John Wayne. Curtiz had the reputation of being a dictator on set, ruling the cast and crew with an iron hand. However, on the set of *The Comancheros*, he was gravely ill, with little energy for such action. George Sherman, who had returned to Moab to produce the movie, helped Curtiz with some of the directing, along with assistance from John Wayne and George White. It was to be his last picture; Curtiz died the following year.

GEORGE STEVENS
Directed: *The Greatest Story Ever Told* (1963)

George Stevens became noted as a director for his drive for perfection and visual authenticity. Born in Oakland, California in 1904, his debut in the entertainment world came at age five, when he began performing on stage with his father's traveling company. Entering the film industry in 1921 as a cameraman, he graduated to directing major features in 1933. George Stevens served as a major in charge of an army film unit during World War II, covering such events as the liberation of Denmark, the freeing of inmates at Dachau, and the capture of Hitler's Berchtesgaden hideaway. Released from the service in 1945, he went on to claim two Academy Awards. The first was for directing *A Place in the Sun* in 1951, followed by *Giant* in 1956.

The Greatest Story Ever Told took Stevens five years to complete. He also produced the movie, which was released in 1965, two years after filming was completed in southeastern Utah. Unfortunately, the critics were not as kind regarding his direction of this film as they were of some of his previous work.

*Blake Edwards, director of 1966 movie **Wild Rovers**, filmed segments around Moab and in Monument Valley. Courtesy of The Academy of Motion Picture Arts and Sciences.*

Director Steven Spielberg selected Arches National Park for the opening scenes of **Indiana Jones and the Last Crusade**.

BLAKE EDWARDS
Directed: *Wild Rovers* (1966)

A native of Oklahoma, William Blake Edwards was born on July 26, 1922, and spent his early years in film as an actor and screenwriter. His start in directing came in 1955 with *Bring Your Smile Along*.

The widely acclaimed *Breakfast at Tiffany's* in 1961, and *Days of Wine and Roses* in 1963, were quite a contrast to *Wild Rovers*, a light Western not released until 1971. Only a portion of the movie was shot in southeastern Utah.

Edwards directed, as well as co-wrote and produced many of his own movies. He created the successful "Peter Gunn" TV series, among others. He directed his wife, actress Julie Andrews, in several films, and also directed and co-scripted several of the *Pink Panther* movies.

RICHARD C. SARAFIAN
Directed: *Vanishing Point* (1971)

Sarafian, a New Yorker born in 1927, was first a researcher for Life magazine. He wrote several scripts in the 1960s and directed for television such successful series as "Ben Casey," "77 Sunset Strip," and "Bonanza."

Sarafian films are characterized by their outdoor locations. *Vanishing Point*, with its highway scenes, and *The Man Who Loved Cat Dancing*, with its mountain terrain, are good examples. His pictures are usually structured around rebel heroes. Considered an interesting director of offbeat movies, several of Sarafian's features have achieved cult status.

EARL BELLAMY
Directed: *Against A Crooked Sky* (1975)

Born March 11, 1917, in Minneapolis, Minnesota, Earl Bellamy became a producer and director of several successful TV series, including "Laredo." During the 1950s and 1960s, he directed occasional low-budget films, mostly Westerns. The year 1975 was a prolific one for Bellamy. In addition to directing *Against A Crooked Sky*, he also did *Seven Alone* and *Part 2: Walking Tall.* Earl Bellamy directed the last Western filmed in Moab until 1993. Science fiction and contemporary adventure scenarios dominated the local scene from 1975 to 1993.

LAMONT JOHNSON
Directed: *Spacehunter: Adventures in the Forbidden Zone* (1982)

A Stockton, California product, Johnson was first an actor. He began directing for stage in the late 1940s and appeared as an actor in several films during the 1950s.

In 1976, Johnson directed *Lipstick*, a somewhat controversial film. His 1980 production of *Cattle Annie and Little Britches* sported a top-rate cast and received excellent ratings.

Spacehunter, Moab's first science fiction movie, was a "3-D" action thriller that proved canyon country could provide excellent galactic landscapes.

STEVEN SPIELBERG
Directed: *Indiana Jones and the Last Crusade* (1988)

Spielberg, the youngest of the directors featured here, was born in 1947 in Cincinnati, Ohio. He was a film enthusiast from early childhood, turning out his first scripted amateur film (with actors) at age 12.

At age 28, he directed *Jaws*, one of the greatest box office blockbusters up to that time. Spielberg has directed numerous movies through the years, nearly all of which have been financially successful. With *E.T.*, he became a millionaire from merchandising spin-offs alone.

Other smash hits directed by Spielberg include *Close Encounters of the Third Kind*, *Raiders of the Lost Ark*, and *Jurassic Park*. Although Spielberg's stay in Moab was brief, he utilized some of the awesome local scenery for the opening scenes of *Indiana Jones and the Last Crusade*. The results were impressive enough to secure screen credits for Utah, Arches National Park, and the Moab Film Commission, and to unfold a new theme for Moab landscapes.

RIDLEY SCOTT
Directed: *Thelma and Louise* (1989)

Scott, born in 1939, favored a film career early in life. Following his attendance at the Royal College of Art and the RCA Film School in the mid-seventies, he became a set designer for BBC Television. From there he moved into directing, with such series as "Z Cars" and "The Informer." In 1967 he decided to try his hand at making television commercials. He and his brother, Tony Scott, have performed well in this medium. Both have directed several commercials filmed on location in Utah's canyon country.

In the seventies, Ridley decided to apply his directing skills to feature films. His movie debut was made with the picture *Duelists* for which he won a Special Jury Prize at the Cannes Film Festival. This was followed by *Alien* and *Blade Runner.*

Sensitive to color and unique effects, Scott was fascinated with the landscapes surrounding Moab. In 1989 he directed the female-buddy "road" movie, *Thelma and Louise*, which was nominated for five Academy Awards. Callie Khouri created the screenplay and walked away with the award in this category. The controversial theme of *Thelma and Louise* has made it a much talked about movie.

WALTER HILL
Directed: *Geronimo: An American Legend* (1993)

Screenwriter/director Walter Hill was born in 1942 in Long Beach, California. He received his education at Michigan State University and initially wanted to be a comic book illustrator.

Prior to getting involved in film, Walter Hill worked in construction and oil drilling. His first film experience came when he served as an assistant director in the late 1960s. Among his first screenplay credits were *The Getaway* (1972) and *The Mackintosh Man* (1973). His first experience as director was for the movie *Hard Times*, which was followed by *The Driver*, *The Warriors*, and others.

"Who's Who in Cinema" describes Walter Hill's style: *Whatever his films' actual setting, they have at their center the conventions and characters of the Western. Hill's style thus owes much to such masters of action film as Walsh, Hawks and Ford.*

Walter Hill brought this spirit and skill to southeastern Utah in 1993, to co-produce and direct the epic adventures of the legendary Apache warrior, Geronimo. The Columbia Pictures feature boasted one of the largest casts ever to be used in Moab-Monument Valley film history.

NOTE: A complete list of directors who filmed in southeastern Utah is found at the end of the "Movies" chapter.

On location in southeastern Utah, director Ridley Scott prepares for filming scene in **Thelma and Louise**. *Photo by Jim Kelly.*

Film Director Walter Hill and John Hagner, founder of the Hollywood Stuntmen's Hall of Fame, on location of **Geronimo: An American Legend** *in Moab. Courtesy of John Hagner.*

BEHIND THE SCENES
WITH MOAB - MONUMENT VALLEY
"REEL" PEOPLE

*Actor Ben Johnson, talking with locals Maggie Taylor and Stella Stewart during filming of **Wagon Master**. Courtesy of The Times-Independent.*

Often the most thrilling, heartwarming, and just plain funny things that happen while making a movie are not captured on film. It may be the director who creates the movie, but it's the people who generate the memories.

Prior to new technology, and before southeastern Utah developed adequate accommodations, stars and crew had to rely more on local folks. Early filming in such remote areas as Moab and Monument Valley meant that film people were usually "put-up" in private homes. This generated closer relationships between the two cultures, and warmth and appreciation became a two-way street. Hollywood soon learned the value of the natives and their creative ability to cope with all aspects of problem solving in their own high desert "backlot." Producing a picture away from the conveniences of the studio was very different. The rugged desert terrain, often threatening climate, and limited access to emergency materials only added to the already monumental challenge of movie making.

Filmmakers have come to respect the talent of local crews. And long after the movies cease to play in theaters, citizens of Grand and San Juan counties can be caught saying, "I remember when..."

MONUMENT VALLEY - The Early Days

The Ringo Kid, Captain Kirby York, Captain Nathan Brittles, Colonel John Marlowe, and Ethan Edwards rode this way; all were in the form and spirit of actor John Wayne. He even named one son "Ethan," after playing the part of Ethan Edwards in *The Searchers*.

When the movie *Stagecoach* was filmed in Monument Valley in 1938, thousands of dollars were paid in salaries to the Navajo people. Every evening as they received the day's pay, they descended upon Goulding's Trading Post to redeem pawn, and stock up on blankets, food and supplies for the winter.

Operating a lodge in Monument Valley was not easy. Supplies had to be hauled from 150 miles away and water, which also had to be hauled in, was always a big problem. Guests were rationed a gallon of water for their personal use, but sometimes Harry and Mike Goulding needed to borrow some of it back before the evening was over.

The year 1940 marked the return of director George B. Seitz, who had discovered the great potential of Monument Valley 15 years earlier when he filmed *The Vanishing American*. This time he was directing *Kit Carson*. There was irony in the situation. The Navajos, who helped to make the movie lauding the Indian fighter, were actually the descendants of the people Kit Carson had pursued into the "place of the monuments" only 77 years earlier.

Work on location can be trying for all involved. The hours spent waiting for the next scene to be shot can get pretty boring. The Native Americans had their own way of killing time between "takes." If they weren't telling each other funny stories about the strange white people shooting the crazy pictures, they were staging horse races off to the side of the set. At night they would gather around camp fires, chanting their songs and dancing. With all that activity in the desert, very few of the Hollywood troops found life boring. And with movie stars and Indians, the tourists who flocked to the area left with some great stories to tell the folks back home.

The movies kept coming, but it wasn't until the winter following *She Wore A Yellow Ribbon* that the Navajos realized the true value of film work. It was the year the snow reached "two Indians deep on level ground" across the reservation. Land travel was brought to a halt, and military planes dropped food and hay to the stranded Navajo people and their livestock. Thanks to John Ford and the payroll he brought to the valley, there were food and blankets in the hogans, and many tragedies were averted.

Every once in awhile, Hollywood's Indians would be brought in for some of the heavier roles. Chief John Big Tree, a full-blooded Seneca, portrayed "Pony-That-Walks" in *She Wore A Yellow Ribbon*. Chief Big Tree was a Hollywood veteran who first worked for John Ford in the 1924 feature *The Iron Horse*. He also posed for the portrait on the Indian-head nickel in 1912.

Ford became so popular with the Navajo that the highest tribute that could be paid to anyone was bestowed on him. While directing *The Searchers*, he was presented with a sacred ceremonial deerskin, complete with ears, tail and legs. The Navajo admired Ford's loyalty and devotion, sense of

Some of Goulding's buildings were used in **She Wore A Yellow Ribbon**, *during early filming in Monument Valley. The rock house in the center served as the quarters of Captain Nathan Brittles (John Wayne). The building and Captain Brittle's sign on the door can still be seen today. Courtesy of The Academy of Motion Picture Arts and Sciences.*

humor, endurance and vitality. For them the award had deep meaning. Printed on the hide was: "We present this deer hide to our fellow tribesman NATANI NEZ," which translates to Tall Leader.

John Wayne was also popular. While in Monument Valley filming *The Searchers*, Wayne became a real-life hero to the Indians. A two-year-old Navajo girl contracted double pneumonia resulting from an advanced case of measles. There was a crew doctor on set, but the girl needed a hospital and oxygen tank. The nearest facility was 100 miles away. Wayne offered his plane to transport the girl to the hospital, which probably saved her life. The Navajos gave Wayne a special name for his deed: "The Man With the Big Eagle."

Several Navajos, cast as Comanche braves in *The Searchers*, received screen credits: Billy Yellow and Bob Many Mules, two of John Ford's favorites, as well as Away Luna, Percy Shooting Star, Pete Grey Eyes, Smile White Sheep, Exactly Sonnie Belsuie, Feather Hat, Jr., Harry Black Horse, Jack Tin Horn, Many Mules Son, and Pipe Line Begishe.

When people on the reservation first learned that the movie crowd was coming, some were reportedly not too happy. "It's goin' to be a sad day when Hollywood comes here raisen' hell," they grumbled. In an interview with Neil M. Clark for the Saturday Evening Post (March 29, 1947), Harry Goulding related an encounter between director Dick Rawson and Hoskinini-Begay that illustrates the good will - not hell - that occurred during the filming of *Billy the Kid*.

An old Indian rode into the trading post one morning when the location manager was hiring Navajos at ten dollars a day to shovel the road. Rawson saw the man standing off to one side, wrinkled, old silver on his wrist, turquoise around his neck, his long hair knotted and tied at the back under his big hat.

"Who's that?" Rawson asked.

"Son of Hoskinini, the last Navajo chief," Goulding replied.

"Why isn't he going to work?"

"He just rode in from the river country."

"Does he need work?"

"Worst way."

"Hey!" Rawson waved to the location manager. "Give this feller a shovel, too."

Hoskinini-Begay spoke no English, but he couldn't mistake the gestures. Later, Dick and Harry were riding past the Indians at work. Hoskinini-Begay left his shovel and came over to shake Rawson's hand. "You tell this man," he said to Goulding, "I thank him for what he told that man."

The movie director and the chief's son were friends instantly, and the friendship ripened and grew. Rawson, since he was short and went bareheaded, was nicknamed Little No Hat. When the picture was finished, he returned to Hollywood and sent Goulding a check for $100, and later another for $250, to help Hoskinini-Begay through a tough winter. Goulding invented errands for the old man to do, to more or less earn the money.

One day the old man came to the trading post with a beautiful white tanned deerskin. He explained that he wanted a message to Rawson written on it, saying he thanked his friend for what the picture people did, providing something for his people to eat and do, and he invited Rawson to return. Hoskinini-Begay signed with his thumbprint, as did many others, at his suggestion. When Goulding personally took the

skin to Hollywood and gave it to Rawson in his beautiful home on the ridge between Los Angeles and the San Fernando Valley, it was more than Little No Hat could take dry-eyed.

Since there was no town in Monument Valley to accommodate the sizable crews in the early years of filming, a huge tent city was erected. In 1963, for *Cheyenne Autumn*, Rolly Harper, of Harper and Green Catering Company from Hollywood, brought in 70 trailers to house the cast, while the crew camped in tents. Twelve thousand feet of water pipe and sewer lines were installed for the temporary town, called "Harper City," and 250,000 meals were served during film production. When the crew moved to Moab locations, Harper City moved right along with them.

Rolly Harper, L.A. caterer brought in for big Western, ***Cheyenne Autumn***. *Courtesy of The Times-Independent.*

NATIVE AMERICAN CONTRIBUTION TO THE CINEMA

John Ford discovered that the Navajo Indians of Monument Valley were not only natural actors who paid off at the box office, but they also contributed to some very special memories. Ford had a tender spot in his heart for the Navajo, and became somewhat disturbed over film scenarios that always depicted Indians in a bad light. A gentle people by nature, the Navajo seem to forgive the way the white man twisted history by nearly always portraying the "redman" as the villain or "savage" in "historical" dramas. In the production of *Cheyenne Autumn*, Ford tried to rectify the situation by showing the plight of Native Americans from their point of view.

Monument Valley is located in one of the most beautiful sections of the Navajo Indian reservation. In addition to the awe-inspiring scenery, a more than adequate supply of Indians stood ready and willing to act in the wild west movies. These Native Americans found the whole movie making game entertaining and sometimes hilarious.

The Navajo Nation has a population of over 180,000 and covers 16 million acres. All filming permits for any location within reservation boundaries (including Monument Valley), must be secured through the land use office at the Tribal capital in Window Rock, Arizona.

During early filming Navajo headquarters were at Kayenta, only 23 miles south of the Utah-Arizona border. Lee Bradley, a Navajo from Kayenta, was one of the first local men involved in movie making. Bradley, who speaks excellent English, began his movie career in 1925 with Richard Dix in *The Vanishing American*. Lee was often hired as an actor, as well as technical advisor and interpreter for all Hollywood studios shooting Westerns in Utah and northern Arizona.

By the time Lee finished work on *Smoke Signal* at Moab in 1954, he had chalked up 57 movies. He had an almost full-time movie career without having been to Hollywood. But then, many others in the Moab-Monument Valley area have discovered that one can become intimately involved with Hollywood without leaving the remote rural environment. For some, this has been the best of both worlds.

Some Navajos have found it amusing that they are almost always cast as anything but Navajos. For example, in the pilot film for the *MacGyver* TV series, 50 Navajos played members of a Mongolian army. And in the 1993 movie about Apache warrior Geronimo, many Navajos played Apaches and some were cast as Mexican Federales.

Fred Cly, location scout for the Navajo Reservation, looks through Tear Drop Arch over Monument Valley, Utah.

Mike Goulding recalled a situation during a production in Monument Valley that reflects the Indians' sense of humor. A young Navajo, playing an Apache warrior, was riding bareback over the sand dunes when his horse suddenly bucked him off. After tumbling down a large coral-colored dune, the young man picked himself up and exclaimed, "If I'd been a Navajo, this wouldn't have happened!"

* * *

Lon Jones, publicist for several of the movies filmed in Moab, sometimes gave an account in the local newspaper of the day's activities on location. Two amusing incidents he reported are included here.

During a dramatic scene staged for **Battle At Apache Pass**, more than 100 Navajos, playing Apaches, were decked out in war-paint and ready to ambush a company of U.S. Cavalry. A section of Courthouse Wash (north of Moab), was doubling as Apache Pass, which is actually located in southern Arizona.

To increase the ranks of the Indians, 20 local Anglos and four Hollywood stuntmen were made up as braves. As director George Sherman ordered "Roll 'em!," the Indians poured down from the hills, firing their guns and shooting arrows. Later, when the cavalry swept into Courthouse Wash, 12 of the young Navajos, dressed in cavalry blues, fought alongside the white men.

"Funny business," one young man from the reservation proclaimed. "I shoot arrow at galloping soldier and miss. Hour later, I play soldier and arrow hit me square in chest. Pretty silly."

For this same movie, actor John Lund was making his first appearance in a super-Western. Fairly excited about it all, he couldn't help but be impressed by the stoic qualities displayed by the unimpressed Indians. Gathering up his nerve, he walked over to a Navajo who was lounging beside one of the wickiups. "How...," he began self-consciously, as the Navajo opened one sleepy eye, "How you make wickiup?"

"Ya got me, Mac," the Navajo replied. "First one of the darned things I ever saw." Whereupon, the Indian rolled over onto one side. Displayed on his shoulder was the tattoo: "U.S. Marine Corps - Semper Fidelis."

* * *

Frank Bradley, brother of Lee Bradley, was also very active in the movies as a technical advisor and interpreter. George White recalled an incident during the filming of **Ten Who Dared** (the John Wesley Powell story), when Bradley brought six Navajo men from the reservation to work in a scene at Dead Horse Point. In this scene, three of Major Powell's crew had deserted, climbed out of the canyon, and were ambushed later at a watering hole. Believing that the Navajos could not speak English, director Bill Beaudine described to Bradley how he wanted the Indians to come out of the juniper trees and make their kill. Bradley relayed the order in Navajo.

According to White, things didn't go too well in the shoot. Beaudine, being somewhat temperamental, flung his hat down, jumped on it and roared, "The ambush is too overzealous!" Beaudine then ordered a retake and told Bradley to have the Indians try again. Bradley said, "Okay boys, come on out."

"I thought they didn't speak English," grumbled Beaudine, after the scene was re-shot successfully. Wanting to keep his job as representative for the Native Americans, Bradley had been afraid to admit that the Navajos spoke perfect English. In fact, two had served as "code talkers" in World War II, where the use of their Navajo language in radio communications had so successfully confused the Japanese code breakers.

As far as Moab kids were concerned, the well-muscled Mohawk brought from Hollywood to play Geronimo in **Battle At Apache Pass** had *their* attention. Other stars, such as Jeff Chandler, Rock Hudson, Susan Cabot, and John Lund, came in a distant second when it came to requests for autographs. The big Mohawk's name was Jay Silverheels, better known as Tonto, the Lone Ranger's trusted friend.

In the same movie, six Navajos were selected to perform the Apache Devil Dance, a pre-battle ritual. Prior to rehearsal, the Navajos were required to watch a film of the actual Apache Mountain Spirits Ritual, photographed at Gallup, New Mexico. The beat, however, was too fast for the Navajo dancers. To solve the problem, an original dance based on authentic Apache steps was devised. Indians who had gathered for the filming of the sequence watched with enthusiasm the dance of the black-masked warriors with their grotesque headdresses. When it was all over, the Navajos made the decision to take the newly devised dance home with them and introduce it for acceptance before the Kayenta Tribal Council.

Not all Native American involvement with the cinema was confined to acting and interpretation. A certain medicine man on the reservation was given an honored place on John Ford's list of essential personnel. Richard E. Klinck, in his book **Land Of Room Enough and Time Enough**, says that Hosteen Tso was one of these people. He was known among the Navajo as "Mister Big," or "Fatso," and also had a reputation as something of a joker.

As the story goes, John Ford had some varied and unusual weather requirements while filming *Stagecoach* in 1938. Harry Goulding first brought "Mister Big" to Ford's attention when the script called for thunderstorms for one day's filming, and the next day he wanted a few snowball clouds in a clear blue sky, followed by a dust storm.

Speaking in jest, Goulding told Ford to just have his weather order in by four o'clock the day before the shoot, and he would have "Mister Big" fix it up. Ford facetiously complied and was startled when he discovered that the medicine man's sorcery seemed to work, for he got his required weather right on schedule.

Ten years later, "Mister Big" was still at Ford's side, proudly managing the weather to meet script requirements for *Wagon Master* in Moab. It appears that a little of filmdom's mysticism and superstition, mixed with a touch of Navajo magic, conjured up an interesting and lasting relationship. Perhaps in today's upbeat industry, Hosteen Tso would simply be referred to as a "special effects technician."

MOAB'S ENCOUNTER WITH HOLLYWOOD

"Moab's people are so different, so genuinely human," said director John Ford during an interview with Margie Stocks and Marjorie Smith. The Moab gals had just attended a journalist's conference in Provo, Utah, and thought they would try out their skills for the local newspaper.

Ford was directing Moab's first movie, *Wagon Master*, and he predicted a great future for the area in the film business. He claimed it was the most perfect location he had ever found, due in part to the fact that Moab's citizens were so cooperative.

The girls also discovered that Harry Carey, Jr. (a star in the film) went by the nickname "Dobe," because of the color of his hair. Ben Johnson, the leading man in the picture, was found to be the modest type and slow to talk about himself. It was his first experience in a lead role. Discovered by Ford, he first appeared in *Fort Apache*, then was given a part in *She Wore A Yellow Ribbon*. Now he was the star of *Wagon Master*.

Johnson had spent his life as a cowboy and once held the world championship for calf roping. Still involved in the rodeo business, Johnson sponsors the Celebrity Calf Roping Contest each year in Ogden, Utah, and was active in Ogden's Western Film Festival. When the author spoke to him at that Festival in 1988, he had fond memories of the people and the good times he had on location in Moab and Monument Valley.

Local Donna Meador Reid was the stand-in for Joanne Dru, the leading lady in *Wagon Master*. Dru had just married actor John Ireland. Although he wasn't in the movie, Ireland accompanied his wife and they considered the stay in canyon country their honeymoon. To kill time while his wife was on location, Ireland hung out at Club 66, playing "panguinee" (a card game) with some of the local guys.

When the moon came up, the stars came out. Town folks and crew members were often entertained by the great accordion music of Danny Borzage and songs of the "Sons of the Pioneers" recording group. Borzage, born in Salt Lake City, had become part of Ford's permanent crew to supply mood music behind the cameras for his Westerns. Ford loved music in his movies and used the "Sons of the Pioneers" at every opportunity.

Dan Borzage, Hollywood accordionist-actor, in familiar pose on **Cheyenne Autumn** *set. Borzage was a favorite of director John Ford and was often asked to play tunes to set the mood for a movie scene. Courtesy of The Times-Independent.*

Before **Wagon Master** filming was completed, Argosy Productions gave Moab an evening to remember. They presented a live stage show at the old high school auditorium (which has since burned down), using their very talented cast and crew. The proceeds, netting nearly $1,000, were used for a special Christmas celebration for the children in Moab. The goodwill gesture was well received by townspeople.

John Ireland helped direct the stage production. When he returned to star in **Sundown** 39 years later, he still remembered what a bad time Ford had given him after the performance, saying that Ireland "was certainly no director." Ireland claimed he had a good time, anyway.

Sons of the Pioneers, often used by director John Ford in his movies.

The author and John Ireland, during the filming of **Sundown: Vampires in Retreat.**

Karl Tangren, longtime rancher and active member of MFC, recalls he was only 19 when he played a Mormon pioneer in **Wagon Master**, trudging alongside the wagon train while carrying a Moab child, three-year-old Kathy Worthington, on his shoulders. As the wagon train emerged from a canyon at Fisher Towers, one of the stars had a single line to speak. According to Karl, the fellow just couldn't get that line right. "Over and over we shot the scene. A wagon train full of action for just one line. By the end of the day that little girl felt like she weighed 200 pounds."

Tangren remembers how hard it was to work with anti-quated equipment and unimproved roads. "There was no highway to Professor Valley yet and it took much longer to get there. Crews often camped at the site. Many of today's popular locations were inaccessible then. But," he added, "they still knew how to put together a darn good movie."

* * *

John Ford returned the following year with **Rio Grande**. People were stunned when he walked through town and greeted, by name, folks that he remembered from his earlier visit.

By the time **Rio Grande** was in full production, the locals were attuned to the Hollywood scene, and the Hollywood cast and crew were able to meld into the community. The glamour had dimmed a little, and movie making was just another job. Many hours, and sometimes days, on location would be spent just waiting for the right cloud formation or weather conditions to match the previous day's shoot.

Film extras killing time between takes.   Photo by Lin Ottinger.

Extras playing cards while awaiting the next call on the movie **Blue**. *Photo by Lin Ottinger.*

To pass time, and to be alert when the production assistant (PA) called: "Everyone on set, let's go!," crew and extras would drum up a card game or just play pranks on one another. According to Jack Goodspeed, a local who often worked as a driver, you didn't dare fall asleep.

Someone would poke sticks in your shoes and set them on fire. Just to be funny, we stuck a potato in the exhaust

pipe of E.A. 'King Fish' Trout's truck, when he delivered grain to the set. When he started the truck, it created a heck of a bang and caused all kinds of commotion.

One day when local Harold Foy was catching a few winks, Bill White (George and Essie's son) and some of the other boys loosened the cinch on his horse's saddle. When the PA said 'let's go!,' Foy woke up, dashed to his horse, jumped on, and over he went, right under the horse's belly. We had a good time, even if it did mean getting called down on set.

Essie confirmed that her son and some of the others were full of the devil in those days. She added, "You might find a burr under your saddle blanket or hobbles on your horse - just about anything could happen."

It seems Ford could be a prankster in his own right. "To get even, he would have the guys believing, right to the last minute, that they had to do without lunch for their shenanigans," said Goodspeed. "Then, when everyone else had been fed, he would let the boys eat."

Many of the locals worked with the film companies during production of both **Wagon Master** and **Rio Grande**. Erma Newell, Sis Taylor, Astell Stewart, Lydia Skewes, Maggie Taylor, and Lelia Turner were among some of the extras hired as pioneer women.

On his birthday, while directing **Rio Grande**, Ford stopped production to throw a party. Scenes were being shot at the Mexican village that day and the event was held on the set. Horse races, foot races, and all kinds of impromptu festivities took place. All was going well until Tommy White (George and Essie's youngest son) was thrown from his horse. Ford called a halt to the activities and closed down the set for the day. He was always concerned about the welfare of his extras and crew. He didn't like to see people hurt or taken advantage of in his pictures.

Rio Grande *set on the White Ranch. Left to right are Essie White, Harry "Dobe" Carey, Jr., Ben Johnson, Claude Jarman, Jr., John Wayne and Maureen O'Hara. Front row is Tommy White, George and Essie's youngest son. Courtesy of Essie White.*

Once in a while, though, especially when large numbers of extras and crew were involved, things would get a bit out-of-hand. George White related one such incident that took place on his ranch during the filming of **Rio Grande**:

The action called for the Indians to raid the cavalry camp, which was set up down in the field near the river. Hoping to catch a special angle of the warriors as they hit the camp, cameraman Archy Stout was stationed behind one of the tents. A Comanche, carried away with the excitement of it all, ran over Stout with his horse, knocking the cameraman out. Stout was taken to the ranchhouse, where the set doctor looked him over and cleaned up his wounds. He was lucky. The damage was minor, mostly cuts and abrasions.

George White recalls the day he and John Wayne went up Onion Creek to check out a location. The "Duke" was shouting "(expletive) Louella Parsons," just to hear the multiple echoes reverberate off the canyon walls. Apparently Parsons, a noted Hollywood columnist, had said something about the actor that he didn't care for, but seems they "goofed off" too long in Onion Creek and, upon returning for lunch, John Ford had the crew remove the sunshade from Wayne's table. George remembers that John Wayne remarked, "The Old Man is getting even with us."

* * *

Battle At Apache Pass was the first technicolor movie made in Moab. Utah's Governor J. Bracken Lee, and first lady Margaret Lee, arrived to extend the state's welcome to the Universal-International cast and crew. While eating lunch on location at Fisher Towers, Mrs. Lee expressed her interest in the sudden growth of Moab as a center of motion picture production work. She invited film officials to consider Salt Lake City for the world premiere when the movie was ready for release.

Mr. and Mrs. D.H. Shields entertained some of the **Battle At Apache Pass** crew with a barbecue at the Red Rock Lodge. At that time, their lodge and the Utah Motel were the two major accommodations in Moab.

Lack of accommodations did not discourage director George Sherman, however. Upon completion of the movie, he stated, "I consider Moab an outstanding location for Western pictures and I most certainly plan to return. The wide variety and startling beauty of your scenic features are without comparison." He continued, "I have seen enough country in the immediate vicinity of Moab to make dozens of pictures without using the same scenic background twice." Sherman did return as promised with two more pictures: **Border River**, and as the producer of the John Ford film, **Cheyenne Autumn**.

* * *

During the filming of **Border River**, a special dinner was held for Sherman, cameraman Irving Glassberg, and others. Also attending were Mr. and Mrs. Beverly Spencer, new editors of *The Times-Independent*, who had taken over after Bish Taylor left to assume a governor-appointed position with the State Industrial Commission. Actress Yvonne De Carlo, star of the film, arrived late for dinner. She had been swimming in the Colorado River with Barbara Burck, daughter of Moab mayor George Burck. "It was great," declared the actress.

At the dinner Irving Glassberg expressed his feelings about how wonderful the area around Moab was going to be

for color pictures. Mrs. Glassberg commented, "We had quite a time today. Just as we were ready to eat our lunch (on location), the wind blew technicolor sand all over our food. The sand was so red, we ended up with pink lemonade."

Joel McCrea was DeCarlo's leading man in **Border River**. When he arrived in town he noticed his name on the marquee of the Ides Theater. The movie was **Lone Hand**, starring McCrea and Barbara Hale. McCrea had never seen the picture, so that evening he and half the crew went to the show. McCrea got a huge kick out of it - much to the disgust of the tourist sitting in front of him. At the end of the movie, as the lights came on, Mr. Tourist turned around to give the gent behind him a piece of his mind. When he realized he was face-to-face with the star of the picture, it cast a different light on the situation. The traveler went home with, "The best part of my vacation was..." to share with all his friends.

"The Duke" kicking in door at Mexican village in **Rio Grande**.

Before the Ides Theater (later the Holiday) was torn down in the early seventies, it was used by film companies to show their "dailies" (recently-shot film sequences). An occasional advance showing of Moab-made movies could also be seen at the Ides. Elberta Clark, who managed the theater, tried to schedule movies starring the celebrities who were in town whenever she could.

Left to right: Unknown, Barbara Rush, Rock Hudson, Barbara Burck and Rex Reason taking a break from filming, at the M-4 Ranch (now Pack Creek Country Inn), then owned by Mr. and Mrs. Rusty Musselman. Courtesy of Barbara Burck Cathey.

According to the newspapers, there was romance in the air. The media proclaimed, "It was first love for Joel McCrea's 18-year-old son Jody and Barbara Burck, the mayor's daughter and stand-in for Yvonne DeCarlo." Jody had his first acting job playing the villain in ***Border River***. When the picture was completed, likewise was the romance, it seems.

This picture was filmed at the peak of the uranium boom in Moab, and 85 percent of the cast and crew had to stay in private homes. Bill Hines and Mayor Burck spent days working out the arrangements. In *The Times-Independent*, director Sherman quipped, "Cecil B. de Mille had gold bathtubs in his scenes, but we have uranium in ours." The film was the first "3-D" movie to be shot in Moab. Many of the crew were held over for the next movie, ***Taza, Son of Cochise***, scheduled to film immediately following.

Barbara Burck continued her movie career by landing a speaking part in ***Taza, Son of Cochise***. Hobnobbing with stars such as Rock Hudson and Jeff Chandler, she also worked as a stand-in, this time for leading lady Barbara Rush. Although Barbara Burck enjoyed the glamorous life, she ultimately decided not to chase after a stardust career. She remained in Moab, occasionally working as an extra on other pictures, and is known today as Barbara Cathey. (Her son, Clay Cathey, picked up where his mother left off. He has not only worked as an extra, but enjoys set construction, mechanic responsibilities, and "grip" work. The grip is responsible for transporting and setting up equipment, props and scenery, laying dolly tracks, and pushing the dolly during filming. The name stems from the fact that one must have a firm "grip" while carrying out these responsibilities.)

* * *

Moab's Arnel Holyoak, who was head wrangler on many area pictures, had occasion to teach a number of the stars how to ride a horse. "Most of the actors and actresses who were cast in roles requiring them to ride had been around animals some," he noted. "But there was one young man that I question had ever seen a horse."

It was during the filming of ***Siege At Red River*** and Holyoak was having a hard time teaching the leading man, Van Johnson, how to stay in the saddle. "Out on set one day," Holyoak chuckled, "the cameras were rolling, Johnson was riding across the flats, and off he flew. The fall ripped open the seat of his pants and shook him up a bit. They had to sew up his britches right out there in the flats."

* * *

Not all accidents happen during filming. Actress Piper Laurie, female lead and the only woman in the 1954 movie ***Smoke Signal***, dislocated her hip while playing softball. Director Jerry Hopper issued firm orders that Miss Laurie cease involvement in any more strenuous games. With several weeks into production, major injuries to one of his stars could hold up the picture indefinitely, at an enormous cost. Fortunately the company nurse, "Doc" Guyer, was on hand and quickly re-aligned Miss Laurie's hip. She was then required to walk for an hour so it would not become stiff and sore. The heat on location that day was stifling (area temperatures reached 109 degrees during this production), but the beautiful young star toughed it out and was back at work that same afternoon.

Smoke Signal was filmed primarily on the Colorado and San Juan rivers. Frank Wright, veteran Mexican Hat riverman, guided the movie company down the treacherous rivers while they filmed. When the major run was completed, which took them from Mexican Hat, Utah, to Marble Canyon Bridge, Arizona, the crew was bestowed with the title "River Rats," joining the elite few who had made the risky journey. The honor, given them by Wright, came complete with engraved certificates to prove they really had made the run.

With the uranium boom still in full swing, *Smoke Signal* star Dana Andrews commented, "It's difficult not to catch uranium fever when you're living and working in the greatest boomtown in the world." During leisure time, the crew bought or borrowed geiger counters and headed for the hills to do their own prospecting. No one was remembered to have struck it rich from these endeavors.

* * *

The first contemporary feature to use Moab as Small-Town U.S.A. was *Canyon Crossroads*, filmed in 1954. Inspired by the uranium boom that began two years earlier, the story centered on the search for riches.

The only paved street in Moab at the time was the state highway that snaked through town, cutting east on Center Street and south on Fourth East. Most of the buildings in the business section were early-century structures, many of which have since been torn down.

Moab's old Cate Equipment Company on Main Street was selected to be the Atomic Energy Commission (A.E.C.) office, an important set in the movie. Fern's Tavern, no longer around, was a location for some of the night sequences. Virginia Johnson, born and raised in Moab, worked as an extra in one of the tavern scenes. She was directed to drink a beer while socializing with others in the pub. An avid teetotaler, Virginia recalled:

You never know what you might be asked to do when cast as an extra. In the tavern shot, I had to really muster my acting ability to appear at all believable. Making it an even bigger challenge, they had to shoot the scene several times before the director was happy with the results.

Arnel Holyoak, local brand inspector and rancher, spent years working as wrangler in the local film industry. Courtesy of Roberta Knutson.

"River Rats" who made the run from Mexican Hat to Marble Canyon for movie Smoke Signal. Courtesy of Clea Johnson.

On location in downtown Moab during filming of Canyon Crossroads, 1954.

48

*Moab women "extras" on set of **The Comancheros**, filmed in 1961. Photo by Gloria Harris.*

*Gloria Harris of Moab as "woman at the well" in **The Comancheros**. Courtesy of Gloria Harris.*

For the movie ***The Comancheros***, a large number of locals were hired, including more women than usual. The vital statistics for the picture also boasts "...an entire tribe of Navajos, who masqueraded as Comanches, were hired." The key location was near Fisher Towers in Professor Valley.

John Wayne brought in his private herd of 22 Texas long-horn cattle, a breed that had become almost extinct at that time. Another point of interest was the two Columbian buzzards caught and trained for use in this film.

What do stars do between takes? Neil Rau, writer for *The L.A. Examiner*, decided to look into the matter. His column on August 20, 1961 reflects some of his findings on the set of ***The Comancheros***. When interviewed, producer George Sherman told Rau:

The Duke here has more interests than any business tycoon I know. He has his own production company, his ranch, interests abroad and all kinds of things to worry about, but when we get a break in shooting he runs to the chess board as though he didn't have a care in the world.

Director Michael Curtiz commented on the activities of stars Stuart Whitman and Ina Balin:

Whitman and his dad are in real estate on the side. And he's over (in his dressing room) with maps, plans and charts up to his ears, figuring out their next housing project. And then I notice Ina Balin, the leading lady in this film, absorbed in a book. Reading is a favorite pastime of many players when they aren't before the camera.

After a long hot day on location, most film crews found all the night life they needed in Moab. While Warner Brothers was in town filming *Gold of the Seven Saints*, a new bowling alley was opened. Actor Roger Moore (known later for his James Bond roles) helped cut the ribbon for the new facility. In addition to bowling and playing pool during their leisure hours, the cast and crew often frequented the various lodges as guests of local members. One such private club was equipped with slot machines and offered a seat at the poker table for those with a desire to gamble. State law enforcement later clamped down on this practice and the slot machines were confiscated, much to the disappointment of some locals and visitors alike.

* * *

A Biblical epic, *The Greatest Story Ever Told*, may not have filmed long in Moab, but it holds the record for the most local people hired as extras and stand-ins for a movie, with 400 strong. The wardrobe department for the picture had 1,000 costumes, with six pieces each. Maxine Newell gave an account of the events in *The Times-Independent*, condensed below.

The day the big scene was shot, Moab was abuzz. Lights blazed in homes all over the valley as residents rushed to make the 4:00 a.m. location call. Stan and Ruth Peck stayed up all night at Arches Cafe, packing more than 500 lunches for the movie troupe.

Many black wigs were distributed to the women of fair complexion, and some of the clean-shaven men were made up with beards. Among the locals hired were Fay Minton, Colleen Taylor, Irene Lowther, Carolyn Wolf, May Minor, and Fay Pruitt. Some were members of Moab's Community Players theatre group, and a good resource from which to recruit actors and extras.

Children were also used in the picture. From the high school there were Judy Clever, Susan Davis, Kenny Latham, Lorna Stoubagh, and others. Betty Jane Gordon, Shirley Velaquez, Diana Foy, Cindy Jackson, Kenny Nelson, and Teddy Purley were among the children selected from the elementary school. Other kids working on set were Tony Fratto, Roger Torres, Freddy Clauser, Albion L. Lawrence, and Librado Gonzales, all of whom claimed movie making was a bit boring, but agreed it was better than school. Wendy Nelson, Moab social worker, was hired to oversee the children on set, and assure compliance with child labor laws. Peggy Pruner did all the record-keeping and cast calls.

The entire Rotary Club, including visiting Rotarians, donned sackcloth garments to work as extras on the film. The group later donated their day's wages to a special fund for the purchase of a new scoreboard at the high school.

* * *

Moab Rotarians dress for the occasion in **The Greatest Story Ever Told**. *Shown in back row, left to right, are: Don Knowles, visiting Rotarians Bill Weitzel and Fred Ray, Larry Norman, Bob Laughery, Wallace Corbin, Glen Richeson and Harold Mueller. Second row, left to right: Les Graves, Cecil Thompson, Bill Teubner, Bill Stobaugh, Ed Claus, Kent Olsen and Forrest Simpson. Front, left to right: Fred Stoye, J.G. Pinkerton and G.A. Larsen. Courtesy of The Times-Independent.*

*"Sermon on the Mount" scene from **The Greatest Story Ever Told**, shot at Green River Overlook, Island in the Sky, Canyonlands National Park. Photo by Lin Ottinger.*

Warner Brothers, filming **Cheyenne Autumn** in both Moab and Monument Valley, hired some Moab wranglers to work with the crew in Monument Valley. One of them was cattleman and movie wrangler, Don Holyoak. "The crew camp was run just like an army barracks, even down to the bugle wake-up and taps for going to bed," reported Holyoak.

Other riders and wranglers were hired from across the border in Arizona. All the riders and horses were used in the scenes and officials had a hard time maintaining control over the situation. Controversies broke out between the union groups from both sides of the state line and a small group of wranglers imported from Hollywood. Arnel Holyoak, head wrangler from Moab, was asked if he could assist with bringing things under control. As Arnel tells it:

There were about 80 head of horses involved in the scene. The Indians got to running races and ignoring the director and those who were calling the orders. I assessed the situation and determined the five young wranglers from Hollywood were causing most of the trouble. Once I identified them, I rode up alongside, caught them under their arms and lifted them off their horses, making clear that the boss was going to bust 'em.

Arnel knew there were going to be some mad people and, sure enough, he was called on the carpet that evening. There were threats of union strikes, but he stood his ground, explaining the problem he had observed and what it would take if they wanted to pull off the scene with all the riders. Film officials listened to him and the boys from Hollywood

were sent home. "Things went remarkably well after that," Holyoak recalled.

In his traditional "get-together" style, Director John Ford threw a "wrap" party when the filming of **Cheyenne Autumn** was completed. The crew in Moab for this picture totaled 350, including the Native Americans from the reservation, one of the largest number ever imported to the area. Cast and crew, including locals, were all invited to the big event.

According to Ford's "regulars," the director loved to throw parties and observe the natural, uninhibited mannerisms of his stars. Then he would often direct them to repeat in a scene something he had seen them do at a film party.

In a newspaper account of the **Cheyenne Autumn** affair, Maxine Newell related some of the evening's activity. The lively party was held at the Desert Inn (now the Ramada Inn). The group danced, sang, and created all kinds of music. Using such instruments as guitars and an accordion, many folks improvised as needed with tableware, glasses, and chopsticks.

Actor Ricardo Montalban proved to be an expert on the bongos, and charmed everyone with his guitar and Spanish songs. Ken Curtis and Shug Fisher, members of the "Sons of the Pioneers" recording group, sang their familiar western tunes, and actress Carroll Baker became champion of the Limbo line. The Duke's son, Pat Wayne, danced the twist with costumer Sherry Wilson, while Richard Widmark kept time with chopsticks. Before the evening was over, the rafters rang with "Oh, Suzanna," as everyone joined in song. "Those were fun times," agree the locals who were involved in the picture.

Moab and Blanding band students pose on **Cheyenne Autumn** *set in Monument Valley. The youths made their film debut as members of the bugle corps in the picture. Shown is Blanding band instructor Douglas Kingdom, who directed the group. Front row: Jack Montella and Darrell Mathews of Blanding and John Cook, Moab. Back row: Bob King, Blanding, and Keith Knight and Mike Henderson, Moab. Courtesy of The Times-Independent.*

Don Holyoak claims his strangest film-related experience occurred during shooting of **Rio Conchos**. Holyoak explains:

Actor Richard Boone had a brother who was a Texas oil tycoon. One day a plane flew over the set, rather low, and all of a sudden hundreds of rubber ducks began raining down on us. There must have been at least 600 of them. There were rubber ducks everywhere! Funniest sight you ever saw. When Boone returned to film **Against a Crooked Sky** *he confided that he no longer let his brother know where he would be filming. He wanted no more rubber duck showers.*

Lin Ottinger was another local gentleman who was active in a number of early movies, as well as later film projects. Ottinger, a long-time tour guide and rock shop operator in Moab, often found himself on set as a jack-of-all-trades. If something broke he could fix it; when something was needed that couldn't be found, he would create it - or a good facsimile. Ottinger climbs like a mountain goat and always has some entertaining stories for fellow workers and visitors.

Fortunately, Ottinger usually had his camera when he was on set. An excellent photographer, he captured some of the best photos the MMVFC Museum and Library has on file. (Many of the photographs in this book are credited to him.)

Professional football player Jim Brown was a great running back for the Cleveland Browns when he made his film debut in **Rio Conchos**. A man with many careers, Brown headed the National Accounts Department of Pepsi Cola Company in New York between football seasons. When in Moab, he had just completed a book titled "Off My Chest," about a series of episodes in his life. Jack Goodspeed of Moab worked transportation on **Rio Conchos**. He reported that Jim Brown wrote articles for the Los Angeles Times, letting them know what was happening on location in Moab.

According to Goodspeed, the extras went on strike for more money during **Rio Conchos**. "All the drivers and wranglers that could be spared were asked to costume-up and go in for the extras. They did, and received an additional $20 for the day." Goodspeed also recalled, "Director Gordon Douglas was pretty good to the crew on that movie. Each night after filming was completed, he would set up a bar on set so everyone could kick back and relax. "The drivers were not allowed to drink the hard stuff," he noted.

Film companies have a history of getting involved in the community's charitable activities. The 20th Century Fox crew was no exception. When the high school drama department produced "Arsenic and Old Lace," a stage had to be built in the gymnasium, which served as school auditorium. The production crew came to the rescue with elaborate furnishings for the stage setting. Propmen delivered and picked up the furniture, and helped to arrange the stage. It was said to look as great as any professional version of the production.

Propmen again saved the day for students when they assisted with decorations for the Junior Prom. The crew provided and mounted heavy brocade draperies around the ballroom, hung huge glass chandeliers, then helped with the construction of a balcony. They even covered a sofa and chair with the same brocade material as the drapes, to go in the ballroom. The result was one of the most elaborate Junior Proms ever staged in Grand County.

In another "good Samaritan" incident, the Harper and Green Catering Company prepared and served a benefit breakfast for the Grand County Jeep Posse, with Miller's Supermarket providing the food. Nearly 400 delicious breakfasts were served, at 25 cents per plate, in a big tent cafe erected by co-owner Rolly Harper. The Jeep Posse made $94, which was used for additional emergency equipment. Mr. Harper also contributed a drinking fountain for Lions Club Park, as well as money to help repair damages caused earlier by vandals.

In a burst of generosity during a smorgasbord leukimia benefit, actor Richard Boone sat for hours in a tub of water, autographing pictures. The photos were then sold to his fans for one dollar, with proceeds going to the leukemia benefit fund. City Market and the Desert Inn were event sponsors.

Richard Boone in bathtub, as stunt to raise money for leukemia benefit. Photo by Lin Ottinger.

The summer of 1967 was big for movie work in southeastern Utah, with Paramount Pictures filming two at the same time. Some 400 enthusiastic residents of Grand and San Juan counties thronged to the Grand County High School, where film officials conducted interviews for bit parts and extras for the Western, *Blue*. About 120 people were hired to work in the film. More were needed later for *Fade In*, the contemporary feature also on-line. Bud Lincoln, head of Grand County Employment Security, and Norman Boyd, chairman of the Moab Movie Committee, helped with the screening. Ivalou Redd, from Monticello, was considered by the company to be the greatest "talent find" of the session. She was given a significant role in *Blue*, and went on to appear in several episodes of TV's "Death Valley Days."

Two major sets had to be built for *Blue*. George White lined up crew people for construction, and Joe Acord was the Hollywood boss over the operation. Marvin Clever and Eben Scharf were retained to oversee the projects. Twelve carpenters were hired to build a Mexican town in Long Valley, northwest of Arches, as well as a set at Redd's Ranch near La Sal, Utah.

*Ivalou Redd on set of **Blue** near Colorado River in Professor Valley. Photo by Lin Ottinger.*

For the first time in Hollywood history, it looked like Paramount Pictures had released two movies before they had finished production. Producer Judd Bernard (*Fade In*) decided to get some advance publicity for his picture. As townspeople and tourists drove past the Holiday Theater (the old Ides Theater), the message clearly lighted on one side of the marquee read: "*Fade In*, starring Burt Reynolds and Barbara Loden," and on the opposite side of the V-shaped sign: "*Blue*, starring Terence Stamp, Joanna Pettet, Karl Malden, Ricardo Montalban."

Since most of *Fade In* was filmed in downtown Moab, it was hard to sort the spectators from the film cast. Citizens and visitors felt they were constantly on candid camera. Company officials, the movie committee and the Chamber of Commerce derived a system for clearance to film various businesses on Main Street. All businesses and homeowners in the vicinity were asked to drop a card to the Chamber, stating they had no objection to their building being photographed. To make it more convenient, prepared statements were available to sign at the newspaper and Chamber offices. According to a report in the paper, the Chamber of Commerce assisted with the filming activities because of the publicity value such a film would net the city. The article stated that Moab merchants had commented on the increase of local business when the movie payroll began. One women's apparel shop owner said she had never been so busy, yet was getting little direct movie business.

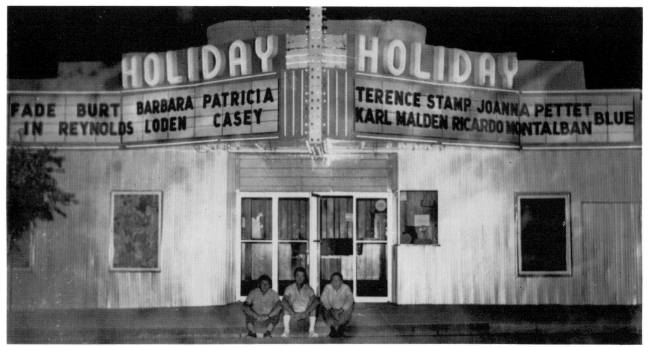

Moab's Holiday Theater, with marquee showing the two movies being filmed in the area. Courtesy of The Times-Independent.

Almost all businesses confirmed that old bills were being paid, often directly with Paramount checks, and some were surprisingly large. Most of the store proprietors volunteered to be on call for services after closing hours. Local motel operators, contacted at the time, expressed delight to have their share of the business. In spite of the fact that many tourists were forced to bypass Moab because there were no rooms available, the movie business was heartily welcomed. Several folks in the accommodations business agreed that what Moab needed was more rooms, not fewer people.

Once production was in full swing, the company filmed **Blue** in the daytime and most of **Fade In** at night. Locals working the night shift as extras included Mr. and Mrs. Eugene Dennis, Lenny Latham, Rick Thomas, Clyde Goudelock, Melba and Kedrik Bailey, John Groff, and Texasgulf official J.G. Pinkerton.

*Moab children working as extras on **Blue**, killing time between takes. Photo by Lin Ottinger.*

Everyone was singing "Take Me Out to the Ball Game" as they gathered around Moab's softball field. The occasion was a softball game, pitting the Paramount troupe against the locals. Stars on the Tinseltown team included Ricardo Montalban, Joanna Pettet, Carlos East, Barbara Loden, Joe De Santis, and Karl Malden. Glen Richeson, Fet McFarland, Corky Key, Russ Donahue, Johnny Cortes, Dan Vlosich, Larry Keyes, Ed Neal, Elmer Dravage, Danny Price, Del Ford and Ron Steele made the Moab lineup. The movie team finally drafted Ron Steele over to their side in a last ditch attempt to improve their score. It was too late - they lost!

Considering the amount of southeastern Utah film production over the years, the area has maintained an excellent record for avoiding accidents, both on and off set. Paramount was not so lucky that year. The company's property master was seriously injured when thrown from a motorbike in a Main Street collision, but later recovered. In a second incident, assistant director Samuel Buchanan was killed in a two-car crash north of Moab, only two days after he arrived. He died in Allen Memorial Hospital of a broken neck. Four Moab men in the second car were injured, but came out of it in good condition. The men were all en route to work with the Circle A Drilling Company. The investigating officer, Bruce Black, of the Utah State Highway Patrol, said Buchanan was traveling at a high rate of speed when his late-model vehicle went into a skid. It was then struck broadside by the second car.

* * *

Ev and Betty Schumaker remember some interesting experiences when, in 1970, they opened their doors to 42 animals and their trainers during the Walt Disney production, **Run, Cougar, Run**. "The menagerie included 22 cougars, 25 Tennessee hounds, two bears, several deer, rabbits, birds, coyotes - you name it," Betty recalled. "They were all kept at our place in Spanish Valley during the six months the company was in Moab filming." The animals were supplied by Lloyd Bebee, well-known animal owner/handler for the motion picture industry.

The animal trainer, Marino Carena, and his wife stayed in a trailer near the animals. It was their duty to keep the creatures calm, while looking after their needs. The cats were maintained in six-foot-square cages and could easily hurt themselves if they got to jumping around. They were located near the gate entrance to the Schumaker home and would usually growl when anyone passed their way.

"One cat was especially bad for growling," reported Betty. "Then one day the trainer explained to me how that particular animal had been trained to growl; it was her special job." Mrs. Schumaker finally got to the point that, if the trainers were gone, she could calm the cats, as needed.

Though several movie stars were involved in *Run, Cougar, Run*, such as Stuart Whitman, Lonnie Chapman, and Harry Carey, Jr., the spotlight was clearly on the animals. Scenes for the movie were filmed throughout Grand and San Juan counties. Moab's Stan Noorlander worked as stand-in for Stuart Whitman.

Animal trainer Marino Carena with one of the big cats used in **Run, Cougar Run**. *Courtesy of The Academy of Motion Picture Arts and Sciences.*

Three cougars were selected for special training to jump from a cliff at Dead Horse Point. To prepare the big cats for the stunt, animal handlers had them leap from Schumaker's roof to the top of a pickup truck. "Each time the animals mastered the jump, the truck was moved further away until it reached the same distance as the cliff jump," Ev Schumaker explained. "After all of the practice, the first cougar lined up for the jump decided 'no way.' The second cat took the entire thing in stride and the director got his shot."

In another incident related by the Schumakers, a cougar was packed all the way to Delicate Arch in a cage. When the crew arrived and set up for shooting, the slickrock was so hot they had to cover it with sand and wet it down so it wouldn't burn the cat's paws.

According to Betty Schumaker, the script created a small problem, calling for mamma cougar to have three kittens, when they usually have only two at a time. "In addition,

cougar kittens grow fast," she noted. "The company was flying in four kittens every few weeks so they would be assured of having three. Each time they would be a little bigger, to match script requirements as the filming progressed.

With six months' filming, Disney Productions was in Moab longer than any movie company on location in the area. They would have remained longer but, according to the Schumakers, a problem arose when the Local Teamsters Union (12 members in all) insisted on driving the vehicles that hauled the animals. Lloyd Bebee and his company liaison, Ron Brown, felt the animals were too valuable to be transported by anyone other than their regular drivers, who were knowledgeable in the special care required to move them. The company was forced to move to Arizona to complete the picture.

The Schumakers visited the crew on set in Arizona, where the company spent another three months in production, and have since made several trips to Bebee's Animal Compound at Sequim, Washington. George and Mary Esther White, also good friends of the Bebees, have done the same.

Run, Cougar, Run was initially planned as a TV movie for "Wonderful World of Disney," but ended up a full feature film. Moab's Grand-Vu Drive-In Theater had a special premiere showing of the movie the following year.

* * *

Until 1991, local realtor Joe Kingsley lived in the Castle Valley cabin used as the Sutter Homestead in the Doty-Dayton Production, *Against a Crooked Sky*. He later added to the structure, but tried to maintain its historical architectural theme in doing so. The original cabin was built by early pioneer Mat Martin, in 1856. Kingsley proudly hosted numerous celebrities at his homestead, since it served as one of the key sets in the Western. Richard Boone had the lead role, playing the part of an old drunken trapper, who hangs out in a cave house near the Sutter homestead. The log entrance to the cave, built by George White, has since been moved to the Hollywood Stuntmen's Hall of Fame Museum in Moab, where it was displayed, just as it looked in the movie.

Moab's Carolyn Dalton doubled for both Jewel Blanch and Shannon Farnon, actresses who play mother and daughter in *Against A Crooked Sky*. Shawn Knutson was stand-in for Stewart Peterson, the Sutter's son, in a few scenes on the river. According to his mother, Roberta Knutson, Shawn remained good friends with Stewart, and they corresponded for several years.

A number of locals landed significant roles as extras. Donald Caldwell, Gordon Couchman, and George Pogue played settlers; Goe Gelo and Roger Darbonne were backwoodsmen, and Eric Bjornstad was a trader, in addition to doubling for Richard Boone, a responsibility also shared by Joe Miller.

Juanita Blackwater, of Moab, was cast as the Indian who assisted Molly (Sutter's daughter) when she returned home with her baby. The infant was played by two-month-old Boyd Ellis, Jr., son of Vicki and Boyd Ellis.

George White again selected all locations, worked with special effects, served as prop man, and also did some doubling. He dressed the set for the Mat Martin cabin and directed the river crossings, with Karl Tangren's help.

Tangren remembers some of the excitement during filming of *Against A Crooked Sky*. A belly laugh tumbles out of Karl as he vividly recalls the scene:

A ladder was set against the eave of the house and star Richard Boone was up the ladder. In between shots he was gazing down at a buxom blonde walking by - and fell right off that ladder.

According to Don Holyoak, **Against a Crooked Sky** had other memorable moments. All the men on set got a "rush" one day when a leading starlet was scheduled to do a nude swim in a small pond at the Kingsley place (Sutter's movie home). The wardrobe lady had a "body suit" (a form-fitting, flesh-colored suit to make the actress appear nude). The starlet proclaimed she didn't need it, quickly stripped, and into the water she went. "Most of the men were about 50 feet across the pond and missed nothing," says Holyoak.

Many of the Navajos working on **Against a Crooked Sky** were seasoned extras and actors, who had played in many of the Westerns filmed in Moab and Monument Valley. Billy Yellow, John Joe Begay, Tim Cly, Denny Yazzie, Charles Betsuie, and David Cly were among them. Moab's Art Manzanares played one of the three Indian braves who rode horseback in the dramatic slow-motion opening sequence filmed in Arches National Park.

Several film companies have utilized the talents of the city police, sheriff's deputies, and highway patrol officers in front of the camera, as well as behind the scenes. The foreign film **My Road**, co-produced by a Los Angeles firm, Dakota Lines, and a Japanese film company named Toho (one of the biggest movie corporations in Southeast Asia), used the officers in their own settings as part of the cast.

The full-length feature starred two of Japan's top actors, Tatsuya Nakadai and Yuhsuki Takita. The plot centered around the exploits of two young Japanese men who backpacked around the United States, learning about life in the states "the hard way." In Utah, their escapades attracted the attention of the Moab Police Department, hence the officers became over-night stars. Moab Police Chief Mel Dalton played the booking officer, Sergeant Alan West (current chief) was the arresting officer, and Grand County Deputy Roy Daughtee received a gunshot during a special scene in the clerk's office.

Karl Tangren, a member of the teamsters union during the Sixties and Seventies, often worked in film as a driver. "I had a fun time driving the little people (midgets) cast in roles for the movie **Spacehunter**," he mused. "I called them my kids." In the film, Karl's "kids" played the inhabitants of the plague-ravaged planet Terra Eleven.

Local Glenn Victor, owner of the Grand Old Ranch House restaurant, provided the catering service for this picture, feeding up to 300 people a day on location. He has also handled the catering for many other film productions over the years.

* * *

An Italian film group making **Choke Canyon** in 1984 found themselves in Moab during Thanksgiving, and residents took them home for dinner. Sheri Griffith, who later became Moab Film Commission president, hosted star Stephen Collins and his friend Faye Grant. Griffith worked with Collins on his riding skills for the movie, in her position as production assistant for the company. Collins and Grant remained in touch with Sheri, letting her know when they got married and again later, when they had their first child.

Choke Canyon offered a real communication challenge, as most of the crew spoke only Italian, or English with a heavy accent. The film commission had its hands full just trying to understand requests and help translate the orders.

Larry Campbell, 1989's MFC president, became quite involved with the vehicle and mechanical side of the **Choke Canyon** production. Finding the right vehicles and modify-

*Director Lamont Johnson (with hand raised, on right) and crew on **Spacehunter** set near Potash Plant. Courtesy of George White.*

56

ing them to meet script requirements is a special skill. Campbell has developed a reputation in the industry for this type of work and was later called to California to fabricate a stealth bomber and various vehicles for commercials and movies. Larry continues to travel to California and elsewhere, usually to do vehicle fabrication or transportation work for the film industry.

* * *

Towns like Moab and Thompson Springs again became recognized in the eighties as good locations for "Small Town U.S.A." In 1985 two companies were in Moab to produce movies. One didn't make it into production and the second feature was released only on video. Lode Star produced *The Survivalist*, and just as the picture was ready for release, problems arose over the title. It was finally released in 1991 under the title *Jack Tillman: The Survivalist*.

When director Sig Shore arrived in Moab, he knew he had his location for *The Survivalist*. When a town becomes the actual backlot for a movie, it involves the entire community. A number of scripts have been written or modified to fit Moab and the surrounding countryside, as was the case with this movie.

Shore confided that there was just one location he might have trouble finding. He wanted a bank building that would allow a bulldozer to crash through the front window. As fate would have it, the Williamsburg Bank was about to be torn down to make way for construction of a new facility. Shore was put in touch with Ron Trimble, bank president, and the deal was made. As it turned out, Ron's daughter, Terra Trimble, was selected through audition to act as the daughter of the lead couple, played by stars Susan Blakely and Steve Railsback. Ron played himself, the banker.

Bulldozer sits ready to bust through Williamsburg Bank window in scene from **The Survivalist**.

MFC staff usually warn film officials up front about the need for their cast and crew to comply with traffic regulations. Perhaps it's because of the fast freeway traffic in California that nearly every company has one or more employees who wind up with speeding tickets. It is often the custom of those ticketed to ask MFC to get it "fixed." MFC's policy says: "You pay just like everyone else!" A lot of embarrassment can be saved when this is made clear right from the start.

Unfortunately, the word was not out fast enough during filming of *The Survivalist*. One of the stars, running late for work, high-tailed it from Moab up the river road (State Highway 128) to Negro Bill Canyon before a deputy sheriff could stop him. The driver's excuse: "But I was late for the morning call!" The officer gave no sympathy. The driver paid his fine and MFC worked to unruffle feathers. Local law enforcement was displeased with the incident, and production was upset when the deputy's car came in behind their star with sirens blaring.

The Virginian Motel became a key location in the movie and Betty Jacobs, motel manager, was most cooperative. Betty has been a strong supporter of the film commission for many years; she was Chamber of Commerce secretary in the Sixties when the chamber assisted the film committee, and was delighted to have them use the motel. During one scene, Moab's Fred Hampton played a "peeping Tom." Hampton usually works as a production assistant or extras coordinator, which he was doing in this picture when the director singled him out to play the part. While he spoke no lines, Fred's expressions were most convincing.

The script called for motorcycles and rough riders. For a while it looked like Moab had been invaded by Hells Angels.

At the same time *The Survivalist* was being filmed, a big-budget movie, *Hot*, began preproduction in Moab. It continued for three months, until one of the major financiers pulled the plug and they had to shut down. Ironically, both companies dropped about the same amount of dollars into local tills.

The best opportunities for locals to gain experience for a film career, in front or behind the camera, is through low-budget, non-union movies. While the work doesn't pay as well as some, it provides for the less experienced to be hired. One of MFC's goals has been to generate local interest in film career development. The presence of talented actors, extras, and crew people in southeastern Utah gives the film commission a competitive edge when trying to recruit a production.

Moab's Allen Memorial Hospital became an important set for filming **The Survivalist**. *Hospital staff became a part of the film.*

*The **Survivalist** crew and extras with director Sig Shore (front, far left), at old Spanish Valley airport, the location used for some motorcycle/vehicle chases.*

By the time director Nico Mastorakis had scouted Arches National Park and Professor Valley for his movie *Nightmare at Noon*, he pleaded: "Don't show me anymore! I'm about to OD (overdose) on scenery." Mastorakis was searching for a small rural community surrounded by scenery. Moab was perfect: "Like the script had been written for it," he said.

Mastorakis took a liking to Sheri Griffith (MFC president at the time), as well as her name. He decided to call his leading couple, played by actors Wings Hauser and Kimberly Beck, the Griffins. He went one step further and named Kimberly "Cheri." Cheri Griffin was just different enough from Sheri Griffith to avoid legal concerns.

The director also changed the town's name from Moab to "Canyonlands," a logical move since the name was prominent on signs about town. It was through the window of the Canyonlands Cafe that one poor actor/stunt person was violently thrown in the movie. When the action was over, the cafe owners got a brand new window.

Several locals had the opportunity to try out their acting skills in *Nightmare at Noon*. Among them were Sheri Griffith, her niece Christy Griffith, western artist Pete Plastow, Dan Mick, now a city councilman, and Nik Hougen, local artist.

Half of the movie was shot in Moab and the rest in Arches National Park, Onion Creek, and Professor Valley. Residents became so accustomed to mingling with production crew that, when MFC scheduled a fundraising basketball game with the stars, one citizen asked: "Why should we pay to see the stars, when we see them daily on the streets."

There were many scenes in *Nightmare at Noon* that required special effects, such as explosions and fire. The company tried to let the public know when and where it would be using explosives. Most of the scenes were filmed at night, when everyone was in bed and traffic was light. Folks were caught by surprise one night when, about 3:30 a.m., a dynamite blast went off that was felt all over town. It is noted that Moab Valley fire officials and equipment are always on set during such scenes.

Actor George Kennedy was so impressed with the area that, after the project was completed, he returned with his family for a vacation. It is not unusual to see movie stars in canyon country simply enjoying themselves.

*On set during filming of **Nightmare at Noon** at the Canyonlands Motel, next door to the Canyonlands Cafe. Both popular film locations are gone, replaced by Best Western Canyonlands and Pasta Jays restaurant.*

* * *

*When John Ireland returned to play a role in **Sundown: Vampires in Retreat**, he had nothing but fond memories from his first visit in 1949. He took a serious interest in developing Moab further as a film center, and was convinced a film lot and sound stage was needed to accomplish this. Ireland concluded that some of the facilities at the Atlas uranium mill, scheduled for demolition, might help the cause, and he hired someone to draw up plans for such a complex. When MFC presented the proposal to Atlas officials, members learned it would be too costly to move any of the structures and most were too contaminated for use.*

John Hagner, the founder of Hollywood Stuntmen's Hall of Fame, tried to get footprints of all stars, stunt people, and other celebrities who visit Moab. When director Tony Hickox was asked to be footprinted, he chose to leave his face print instead.

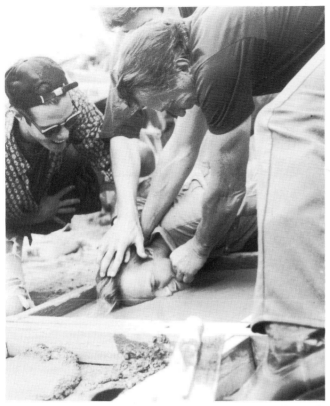

Director Anthony Hickox being "face" printed at the Hollywood Stuntmen's Hall of Fame in Moab.

Sundown star, Debra Foreman, loved quilts. Ray Tibbetts, a local realtor who played a vampire in the movie, took Debra to one of his wife Caroline's quilting bees. Fascinated with the process, Miss Foreman bought a beautiful quilt for her mother. Tibbetts knows that celebrities appreciate extracurricular activity while on location. He and others have been available over the years to take them fishing, hunting, or whatever suits their fancy. Some lasting relationships have been formed in this manner.

David Carradine sponsored the *Sundown: Vampires in Retreat* cast party as a fundraising project at the Sundowner Restaurant. It netted $546.70 for Susan Miller's Grand County Middle School Art Department. Carradine's wife, Gayle, promoted the project.

* * *

Security is tight whenever a big-budget feature - with big names - is considering southeastern Utah as a location. When MMVFC is contacted by such a company, staff is asked to have a complete media/information "blackout." Problem is, most people with these projects leave the film commission office and go about town telling everyone from store clerks to the motel desk manager why they are in town. Although MMVFC people remain mum, there are no secrets in southeastern Utah. More than once, MMVFC has been wrongly blamed for leaks of information, such as when *Indiana Jones and the Last Crusade* came to town.

Director Steven Spielberg had chosen Mesa Verde National Park for opening scenes in the movie. The art department spent several months planning the set for this location. Only weeks before the production was to arrive for filming in southwestern Colorado, an environmental movement brought the use permits to a halt. The company was hard pressed to replace this important location, with little time to do so. The clock was ticking and tension was high when the location manager reached Moab and, silent though MMVFC staff was, it didn't take long for townspeople to know why he was here. Areas of Arches National Park were finally approved as comparable to the former site. What Arches lacked in Indian ruins, it made up for in awesome scenery. The cave and ruins were constructed on set in California, and blended convincingly into the scene.

Following *Indiana Jones* and the blockbuster *Thelma and Louise*, film business really picked up in canyon country. Without question, these movies had an impact on tourism as well. Many travelers went out of their way to see where these pictures were made. There was even a series of special tours, arranged by out-of-town agencies, that took fans to *Indiana Jones* locations.

One lady from Texas marched into MFC's office and

*During the making of **Sundown**, some strange-looking creatures roamed the streets of Thompson Springs - or "Purgatory," as it was called in the movie. Courtesy of Jim Kelly.*

requested a "male" guide to take her to every location where *Thelma and Louise* was filmed. Staff was a bit reluctant, considering the alleged "male bashing" theme of the movie, but managed to find a willing man who toured with the woman - and returned safely. With "movie mania," one can never tell what might happen.

Shannon Lavender Rowe, a local extra, bit player and production assistant, was delighted to hear that Geena Davis would be in Moab to star in *Thelma and Louise*. The two women spent their freshman year as students at New England College in Henniker, New Hampshire, and at the overseas campus in Arundel, England. Shannon recalled:

We lived on the second floor, across the hall from one another, at Colby dorm. We took various theater classes together. For college theater credits we performed at the Muddy River Playhouse during lunch hours. We called it the Lunch Box Theater.

It was during this time that Geena had the lead in the musical "Company" and played a character named April. Ironically, her big break into motion pictures came with Tootsie, *starring Dustin Hoffman, where she played a girl named "April."*

Our dormitory floor was like a girl's slumber party, the camaraderie was always there for a sister. In her character, Thelma, Geena plays much the same kind of person I knew in college. Her role was described as "always easy-going and thoroughly lovable."

Geena Davis and Shannon Lavender Rowe during filming of *Thelma and Louise*. Courtesy of Shannon Lavender Rowe.

Thelma and Louise became a modern-day classic. Controversy raged on whether the picture celebrates liberated women, male bashers, or outlaws. Women especially enjoy the movie because it seems to release pent up frustration felt toward chauvinistic, obnoxious, vulgar, or overly aggressive males. It is as though *Thelma and Louise* accomplished something women wished they had done in similar encounters with the male gender - but never dared.

As reported in Time magazine (June 24, 1991): "It remains the most intriguing movie now in release. No other cheers one's argumentative spirit, stirs one's critical imagination, and awakens one's protective affection in quite the way *Thelma and Louise* does."

* * *

For movie *Thelma and Louise*, hundreds of men, women, and children answered the call for extras.

Moab landed a cyborg flick called *Knights*, starring Kris Kristofferson, in 1992. The casting call for extras attracted about 300 people. One fellow even brought his pet boa constrictor along. The first assistant director (AD) and casting director, Kelly Cantley, interviewed hopefuls, telling each person that they would be working long hours in a very hot desert setting. She asked if they felt they could handle those conditions. Most locals seemed offended and assured her it would be no problem. After all, they lived in this environment. What they didn't know was that they would be costumed in several layers of clothing, and that July temperatures would be higher than normal for more days than usual.

On a day when the temperature rocketed to 115 degrees, a sizable number of extras were on set. By evening, several people were in the hospital with heat prostration. The production company had to make some fast adjustments. Officials saw to it that there were more fluids on set, with assurance that all crew, actors and extras drank frequently. Additional shelters were set up to provide shade. Extras were allowed to bring umbrellas, for further protection when they were not in front of the camera.

The incident caused quite a stir, and union, state and federal officials began dropping by the set to check things out. Included were Occupational Safety and Health Administration (OSHA) and state health officials, a representative from the Utah State Industrial Commission, as well as others from SAG, and the teamsters. This served as a good reminder that the climate in canyon country can wreak havoc on a production if proper measures are not taken. The company made the necessary corrections. In addition, film execs improved conditions by filming a few days in the desert, then moving into the nearby La Sal Mountains where it was much cooler.

*Local rock climber, grip, and photographer, Bego Gerhart, with actor Bruce Boxleitner. Gerhart did the rigging for second unit on TV movie **Double Jeopardy**. Courtesy of Bego Gerhart.*

Film commission staff is accustomed to calls for help at any time of the day or night. Kari Murphy, MMVFC assistant director, had become a proficient troubleshooter for such conditions. Her phone rang at 9:00 p.m. It was the **Knights** office coordinator, all in a dither. "We need a nursing mother with child, as extras for tomorrow's a.m. call," said she. "Where can we find one willing, on such short notice?"

Kari smiled, and turned to query her friend, Teresa Randall, who just happened to be sitting across the room, nursing her 6-week-old daughter, Molly. Back on the phone, Murphy assured the caller that mother and child would be up bright and early to make their film debut.

It is often chancy having a small child on set, since they sometimes decide to cry just as the director calls, "Roll 'em." In Molly's case, the problem was reversed. They couldn't get her awake to nurse during the scene. Mother and daughter were kept in an air-conditioned trailer until time to go before the camera, and were released directly after their scene was shot. This made baby Molly the youngest extra ever to work on a film produced in southeastern Utah.

* * *

As the years roll by and the world becomes more hectic, with more people moving ever faster, folks aren't as inclined to take the time to look, listen, build relationships, care. In analyzing several decades of the film experience in remote Utah, one sees considerable change. Today, most big-name, big-budget movies are "closed" sets - with a capital "C." It seems information about a production is more "classified" than Secret Service files. Society's "let's sue" attitude may be at least partially to blame. Adding to company concerns are the hordes of tourists who frequent most areas where film officials want to shoot.

*Group of local extras pose during filming of **Knights**. Photo by Vicki Barker.*

Only occasionally do you get an honest-to-goodness "down home" star on set. It is rare to hear a truly caring story. In 1993, Columbia selected Moab as its base for the big movie *Geronimo: An American Legend*. It was during this three-month-long production that a few things occurred reminiscent of earlier days. Could it simply be the type of people attracted to work in a good old-fashioned Western?

Robert Duvall, who plays a salty old Indian scout, Al Seiber, in the *Geronimo* flick, was about as down home as a celebrity can get. He radiated good will for the company wherever he went. According to many stories that circulated about town, it was hard to distinguish him from the residents. A local mail express person, delivering a package to an occupant at a local motel, advised the desk clerk that she had a package for Robert Duvall. A man behind her responded, "Here I am." She had him sign the receipt log and was halfway down the street before she realized whose autograph she had just acquired.

Duvall frequented most downtown businesses and would show up at socials when invited, so long as his shooting schedule didn't conflict. He was a willing subject for both photograph and autograph seekers.

Not long after some 250 crew members arrived to begin *Geronimo*, one of them was peering from his rear window at the Super 8 Motel. He chanced to observe a lady backing out of her driveway across the street. The anonymous observer stood helpless as he watched her back over a tricycle. The small lad who owned the tricycle was in tears and the mother raged at him for leaving it there. "Humility" is the only word that can express the mom's feeling next morning, when a glistening new tricycle was delivered to her door from an anonymous donor with the Columbia Pictures crew. And, of course, the little boy now believes in "trike fairies." The mother was Kari Murphy, assistant director of the Moab Film Commission, but there was no way the donor could have known that at the time.

With closed sets, where public roads cut through the middle of a film location, it is always more difficult to control access points. The *Geronimo* location, near Shafer Trail below Dead Horse Point, was this type of set. The Shafer Trail is popular with area visitors, although traffic is infrequent.

One day a tourist became disoriented and wound up in the middle of "base camp" (where crew people are fed, stars rest, and extras are costumed). When Larry Campbell, assistant location manager, tried to redirect the tourist out of the area, the gent became angry. It took several rounds before the man and his female companion were on their way in the right direction. The visitor later wrote a letter to the editor of the local paper claiming he had been purposely diverted to the base camp so the crew could sell him *Geronimo* souvenirs. This was quite confusing to Larry and others on set, until they realized that some pranksters in the props department had tacked a sign on the back of the prop truck where they had a bunch of junk from dismantled sets. The sign read: *"Geronimo* Souvenirs For Sale."

Movie publicists no longer write columns for the local papers, nor will they, in most cases, allow the media on set to do their own stories. Everything is "strictly confidential until the picture is released." And they are highly protective of their stars. During Moab's "Butch Cassidy Days," the rodeo committee tried to get permission from Columbia for actor Wes Studi, who plays Geronimo in the movie, to ride in the parade. Although it appeared impossible, on the designated day Studi was there heading up the parade as grand marshall. When the publicist was later questioned, she stated, "Oh, he did that as a citizen, not as a star, and that's all right."

Ellie Inskip of Moab worked as liaison between Columbia, MFC, and Grand County Job Service. This picture was so big that Job Service Director Ken Curtis funded a position to relieve the extra workload anticipated for the MFC office. Inskip was allowed 400 hours to assist casting in the selection of local extras and bit part players.

*Native Americans working as extras in **Geronimo: An American Legend**. Courtesy of Tony Benally.*

Local extras on "Fort San Carlos" set for movie **Geronimo: An American Legend**. *Courtesy of Mary Engleman (center).*

Numerous locals were used as bit players or extras in close-ups - often in death scenes. Moab's Art Manzanares portrayed a Mexican Federale killed by Geronimo in a dramatic death scene. Art, who is of Spanish descent but doesn't speak the language, was directed to plead for his life as Geronimo readied for the kill. Manzanares was bent on not losing this opportunity just because he couldn't speak Spanish. He began gibbering non-words with terror in his eyes. Director Walter Hill was impressed enough with his acting to keep the shot, but unfortunately it did not make the final edit.

Moab's Lance Christie and Robin Sheridan played dead prospectors, and Nik Hougen took part as a stagecoach driver. Shannon Rowe played a way station cook.

Davina Smith of Blanding received praise for her performance as an Apache woman, clutching her baby in horror as she witnessed the cavalry hanging her Apache husband at Fort San Carlos (in Professor Valley.) Her scream was so believable it sent shivers through the crowd of extras. The baby was 11-month-old Amber Many Goats, daughter of Mr. and Mrs. Jim Many Goats of Nazlini, Arizona. (Scene cut.)

Hundreds of Native Americans were screened for **Geronimo**. Because of tight production schedules, film companies are always anxious when using Native Americans, who are noted for their own way of measuring time. All who were hired on the picture were reminded over and over about the importance of being on time for early morning calls. There was a standard joke among the Native Americans, reported Ellie Inskip. It goes: "What does an Indian man *never* say to his wife?" Answer: "Hurry honey, or we'll be late."

Once Columbia completed the on-location portion of the picture, many of the extras and local crew members came into MFC's office to sign up for the next picture. One very mean-looking Native American, Johnny Johnson from Montezuma Creek, walked in and asked for a registration form. The author studied him, thinking he should do well; he had a hostile appearance, a look usually desired for Native Americans in Western films.

When MFC personnel took a polaroid photo to include with the registration form, Johnny looked just as angry and the author commented, "You look good and mean." To this,

Johnson replied: "For weeks they have been telling me, 'Look mean, look mean'!" With a big sigh, he continued, "It's going to take me months to stop looking mean!"

* * *

Castle Rock Productions arrived on the heels of Columbia, ready to shoot *City Slickers II: The Search for Curly's Gold*. Because of the time required for processing permits to film on BLM land, Castle Rock's location manager, Rick Dallego, sought private land for as many locations as possible. Heidi Redd's Dugout Ranch, in Indian Creek Canyon at the entrance to the Needles District of Canyonlands National Park, was selected as a key location and Heidi made the perfect hostess. She had worked with small commercial productions, but none compared to the crew, equipment and livestock that bombarded her place on this production.

John and Nancy Hauer, from South Dakota, had purchased prime land in Professor Valley. On this property they constructed a house so unique that it made the cover story in Architectural Digest (May 1993). The home is built between enormous red rocks, near where the fort was constructed for the early Western, *Smoke Signal*, and later used for *Siege At Red River*. A huge plate glass window, set in rocks, faces a fantastic vista with Locomotive Rock and Fisher Towers. John and Nancy have become "movie buffs," and enjoy the area's film history. They have videos of many of the Western movies filmed on their land, and John can point out exactly where each scene was shot. The Hauer property is still being used for film projects.

The Hauers are horse people and enjoy taking stars and other celebrities horseback riding. When *City Slickers II* arrived, John and his daughter Kyla had the pleasure of escorting stars Billy Crystal and Jon Lovitz, along with Billy's personal horse trainer, on just such an excursion.

Along the trail, Hauer noticed his guests grouped and studying something on the ground. Approaching them, he discovered the object of interest was a three-foot long bull snake. Dismounting from his horse, John gathered up the snake and asked the men if they would like a closer look. "They were quick to let me know they had seen enough," said Hauer.

On Location with **City Slickers II: The Search for Curly's Gold**, *at the Dugout Ranch in San Juan county. Photo by Leo Dutilly.*

Hauer heard that, following this incident, Billy Crystal put out a call for a snake wrangler. An area resident just happened to have a cousin visiting who was one, and was looking for temporary work. He even had his "snake stick" with him. The gent was hired and assigned to clear each location of all snakes before the company arrived to film.

Castle Rock Productions on location in Professor Valley for **City Slickers II**. Photo by Leo Dutilly.

Heidi Redd in front of her tack shop at the Dugout Ranch, with local mountain man Monte Swasey (L) and ranch hand Delmer Titus (R).

Billy Crystal does his own riding in **City Slickers II: The Search For Curly's Gold**. Photo by John Hauer.

Actor Ted Danson and U.S, Humane Officer, Lynn Stones of Moab. Stones was looking after the welfare of a snake used in **Pontiac Moon**. Courtesy of Lynn Stones.

John Hauer also spent considerable time showing director Simon Wincer the country on horseback. Wincer was in town filming some action sequences for the Paul Hogan Western, **Lightning Jack**. His previous credits include **The Man From Snowy River** and the television series "Lonesome Dove." As John and Simon rode through Onion Creek and Professor Valley, Hauer learned that Wincer was a real fan of John Ford and John Wayne. "He enjoyed riding the coun-

try where these men had filmed before," said Hauer.

One of the **Lightning Jack** scenes was shot near Fisher Towers, with about 30 Indians storming off a steep hill, riding bareback. The area was rough and rocky and three of the riders fell off. One was sent to the hospital with minor injuries and the rest mounted up for another "take." Other scenes for this picture were shot in Valley of the Gods, near Mexican Hat, Utah.

WHEN LOCALS GO ON CAMERA
FOR MORE THAN JUST ATMOSPHERE

There may be no better place to get a chance at stardom than in southeastern Utah. The guys and gals shown here represent only a small number of local folks who were selected for special roles in motion pictures. A couple of them landed feature roles, others bit parts, and a few had only dramatic close-ups on camera; all got a kick out of the experience. To date, only one went to Hollywood to further develop a career.

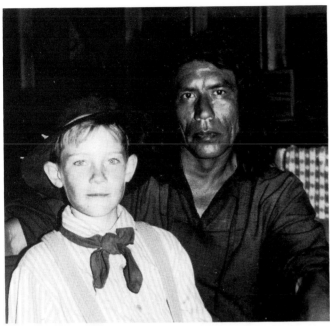

Local Justin Lavender has won roles in "America's Most Wanted," several commercials, and is often selected as a principal extra. He is seen here with actor Wes Studi on set of **Geronimo: An American Legend.** *Photo by Shannon Rowe.*

Ivalou Redd of Monticello played the role of Helen Buchanan in the movie **Blue,** *filmed by Paramount in 1967. Courtesy of Bud Lincoln collection.*

After working as a stand-in for actress Barbara Rush in **Taza, Son of Cochise,** *local Barbara Burck was chosen for a speaking role in the feature. The above photo shows her death scene. Barbara was also a stand-in for Yvonne DeCarlo in* **Border River.** *Courtesy of Barbara Burck Cathey.*

Ivalou Redd attributed her motion picture and TV career to Moab, and to Bud Lincoln in particular. It was he who brought her to the attention of Paramount Pictures during the filming of **Blue.** When the company took her to Hollywood to complete the picture, she met Robert Stabler, producer of the television series "Death Valley Days." Stabler promptly cast Ivalou as Mary Brown in the segment "Britta Goes Home." Impressed with her talent, he gave her other roles in the series. These included: Mary Lake in "Dress for a Desert Girl," Eunice Wilson in "The Secret of the Black Prince," and Cora Stewart in "A Key to the Fort." On April 13, 1975, just as her star was rising, Ivalou Redd died from a sudden illness at her home in Monticello.

Every once in a while, a movie hits town that provides a number of opportunities for local actors. **Nightmare at Noon,** about a small western town that has its water supply poisoned, was one such picture. Several people were cast in challenging roles.

Artist and actor Nik Hougen played a stagecoach driver in the 1993 **Geronimo** feature. Nik is often selected for bit parts in area movies, such as **Nightmare at Noon**, in which he was cast as a country guy who gets shot full of holes and pushed, truck and all, into Ken's Lake. Courtesy of Nik Hougen.

River runner and expedition outfitter Sheri Griffith plays an enraged mother who tries to kill her young daughter in **Nightmare at Noon**.

Castle Valley's Pete Plastow, noted western artist, put down his paint brush to play a crazed priest in **Nightmare at Noon**, shown here with actor George Kennedy.

Vanessa Pierson won a principal role in **Sundown: Vampires in Retreat**. Asked if she wanted a movie career, Vanessa said, "No, I would rather be a veterinarian." Courtesy of Yvonne Pierson.

*Moab Film Commission founder George White was given a speaking part in the Disney picture **Ten who Dared**, 1959, the story of John Wesley Powell's river expedition down the Colorado.*

*Moab's Art Manzanares was a principal extra in the opening scenes of **Against A Crooked Sky** (above), and snagged a bit part in **Geronimo** as a Mexican Federale. Courtesy of Art Manzanares.*

While these photographs represent only a few of the residents who have landed roles in movies filmed locally, it shows how opportunity can be found by those who are interested. Unfortunately, not all hopefuls make it through the cutting room. It is not uncommon to have entire scenes wiped out when the film is edited. This is simply a risk of the business. Most actors feel the experience is well worth the risk, as they will likely be more confident in the next audition.

*Blanding's Davina Smith played the wife of "Dead Shot" in **Geronimo**. Most of Davina's scene was cut from the theatrical presentation, but she has been advised that her part will be put back in for the video release of the movie. Courtesy of Davina Smith.*

THE UNSUNG HEROES
OF THE BIG SCREEN

This chapter is a tribute to the men and women who risk their lives bringing thrills and chills to audiences, those who perform the daredevil stunts in film, but who, for many years, received little or no credit. These professional stuntmen and stuntwomen are truly appreciated for their contribution to the entertainment world.

Stunt work for **Battle At Apache Pass**. *Courtesy of Academy of Motion Picture Arts and Sciences.*

It was 1953 and the scene was a landscape of unique rock formations a few miles north of Moab, known today as Arches National Park. The movie was **Battle At Apache Pass**. It had been a typical location day, with hours of patient waiting, waiting for the clouds to form a reasonable facsimile to those gracing the sky when cameras shut down the day before.

Suddenly an assistant director barked over his bullhorn for everyone to: "Take your places!" The sky was right, the pressure was on. Both extras and crew hustled to their assigned positions. Companies were more lenient in those days about visitors on set and observers were pushed back to a safe distance behind the cameras. The scene about to be filmed involved a stunt, with horse and rider, and stunt work always produced more tension on set.

"Lights! Camera! Action!" Breaths caught as horse and rider rolled head-over-teakettle down the steep 30-foot slope, landing in a heap in front of the camera. "It's a take," declared the director. Chuck Roberson, the top-notch stuntman who had taken the fall, enjoyed the sound of those words.

Roberson, like others in his profession, always tried to get it right on the camera's first roll. The second participant in this precarious shot was a California trick horse, and you

can bet the horse was just as pleased that the scene went well.

From the very beginning, folks in Moab and Monument Valley received a real education as to what goes on behind the camera. How they viewed the cinema changed radically for those who worked with movie crews. In the theaters, they no longer tensed up with suspense when a wild stallion trampled a fair maiden. More likely they would laugh. They knew the prop man was just off-camera with look-alike horse legs on a pair of sticks. When the director yelled "Action!" the prop man would manipulate the legs, with hooves pounding the poor girl into the ground. Movie audiences, caught up in the drama, would be convinced of her impending death. Of course, the fair maiden in the scene was not the young starlet, but her stunt double.

Stunt work demands extreme skill and knowledge, perfect timing, and a cool head on a set where most of the crew is operating at high anxiety levels. The scenes in which the stunt people perform are usually the big adventure/action sequences of a movie. Often they are doubling for the stars in the picture. Herein lay the problem of why so little was known about those talented men and women for many years. Studio executives, in the early days of Hollywood, felt that acknowledging stunt people would damage the image of their stars, an image in which much time and money had been invested. When it came to giving credit, therefore, the men and women who performed the stunts were perhaps the most neglected. Only in recent years have these brave souls received the screen credits they deserve.

Many Hollywood stars began their careers as stunt people. Some made it to the big time, while others spent a lifetime playing minor parts, usually involving stunt work. Ben Johnson and Burt Reynolds are two stuntmen who succeeded as stars, and both were lead men in Moab-based movies.

*The "Duke" and his stunt double, Chuck Roberson, take a break during the filming of **The Comancheros**, near Moab. Photo by Gloria Harris.*

Chuck Roberson preferred less limelight. He continued as a stuntman, but was often cast in small roles at the same time. Considering the number of movies he made in Moab and Monument Valley, he was all but a resident of the area. In addition to his work in **Battle At Apache Pass**, he played a cavalryman in **Rio Grande**, juror in **Sergeant Rutledge**, platoon sergeant in **Cheyenne Autumn**, and served as the stunt double for John Wayne in **The Comancheros**.

Yakima Canutt was another stunt great to visit the area, first in **Stagecoach** in Monument Valley, then **Blue** in Moab. Canutt was the second unit action director on both pictures, using his stunt experience to plan and direct the major battles. Moab's George White performed occasional stunts in those days. He worked with Canutt on **Blue** and remembers it as a valuable experience. Canutt's son, Harry "Tap" Joe, and Jerry Gatlin were also key stuntmen in **Blue**.

Cliff Lyons, another stuntman who played occasional minor parts, worked most often as Ford's second-unit director. Lyons was cast as "Red Shirt" in **She Wore A Yellow Ribbon**, the same character played by Sal Mineo in **Cheyenne Autumn**.

George White's eyes twinkled as he recalled a scene in **Siege at Red River,** that required stuntman Al Wyatt to jump from a 20-foot ledge onto a cavalryman riding below:

"Wyatt, dressed as an Indian, bulldogged the soldier from his horse. They rolled on down the slope, coming to a

stop with the soldier smack under Wyatt. Thinking he had killed the poor guy, he shook him and asked, 'You all right?' As it turned out, he was only stunned from the rough-and-tumble maneuver."

According to White, the Indian siege, which took place around the fort constructed at Locomotive Rock in Professor Valley, was filled with spectacular falls and fights, all performed by excellent stuntmen.

A lot has been said of stuntmen, but what of stuntwomen? When things became really wild in the early Westerns, stuntmen often donned wigs and dresses to perform the risky action. The scene would be staged far enough away from the camera so viewers wouldn't be able to tell the difference. Essie White said one of the funniest sights she ever saw was local Harold Foy dressed as a woman, to handle wagon and team.

"It was in between takes, and Harold was standing under a tree biding his time. Nonchalantly, he lifted his skirt and pulled out a pack of cigarettes, then hoisted up his blouse to get his matches. Lighting his cigarette, he strolled off, unaware of how funny this looked to others."

When John Ford discovered that Essie could ride horseback, he asked her to do a scene in **Wagon Master** that required a fast gallop away from the camera. Essie gave it her all, and so did the horse. Running away with her, the panicked horse charged over a steep embankment to land on a ledge below, where they both teetered precariously until rescued.

In the same movie, Essie rushed into the Colorado River with actor Ward Bond. In the scene, they had traveled far and were very thirsty. Gentleman that he was, Bond scooped up a hatful of muddy river water and offered Essie a drink. With cameras rolling, she dared not falter, and downed every drop. Recalling the incident, Essie noted, "That had to be one of the worst things I was ever called upon to do in the movies. The dirty water was awful-tasting."

When Ford returned to film **Rio Grande**, Essie White was asked to stand in for leading lady Maureen O'Hara. (A "stand-in" is someone who stands in for the star while the lights and camera are being set up for the next shot.) This did not require union membership. To be a "double," however, *did* require membership in the union. A double is one who takes the place of the star on camera, usually in scenes that involve stunts or are far enough from the camera that the double can't be recognized as anyone but the star. It was not unusual for stand-ins to be asked to double, but they always had to be referred to as a "stand-in" because of union rules. Such was the case with Essie White, when she was asked to take O'Hara's place in a runaway wagon.

Essie White was strapped in the front seat next to a stuntman who appeared to have control of the reins. The action called for the stuntman to jump onto the horses and bring them to a halt, once they started to run. Another man, out of sight behind Essie, actually had control of the reins. The director called for action, and the horses and wagon careened through the flats. All seemed to be going as planned until the stuntman jumped to bring the horses under control - and the reins broke. "Those horses really turned loose then," Essie declared. "The stuntman managed to get to the tongue of the wagon and drop free and clear. I would have cleared the wagon too, if I hadn't been strapped in."

While Essie was doomed to ride it out, a fast-acting crew came to the rescue. Driving a couple of vans, used to transport crew and extras to location, they raced to catch the runaway team. As the vehicles closed in on both sides of the wagon, local cowboys and Hollywood stuntmen were stationed ahead to stop the team, which they managed to do.

John Ford came running. "Were you afraid, Mrs. White?" he asked. "No," she replied, "I've been around horses all my life and it would take a lot more than this to scare me." According to Essie, she really did feel calm when Ford confronted her with the question. But a few minutes later, when the reality of the incident finally hit, she "almost fell apart at the seams."

May Boss was one of the few Hollywood stuntwomen who worked on early Westerns in southern Utah. She doubled for Virginia Mayo in **Fort Dobbs**, and was required to ride a horse into deep water in the Colorado River, lose her horse, and swim downstream. Witnesses claimed she did a superb job.

On the set of TV's **"Alias Smith and Jones"**, a stunt double was brought in for actress Marie Windsor. Following a few rounds of unimpressive stunt riding, the gal was sent back to Hollywood. After that, Windsor, a native of Marysville, Utah, and an excellent rider, did her own stunts.

Adventure films, such as **The Eiger Sanction**, filmed in Monument Valley, required the additional skill of rock climbing. Professional mountain climbers Mike Hoover and Peter Palfian were brought in to do the job. Moab rock climber Eric Bjornstad served as a technical advisor and also made climbs of the famous Monument Valley rock spires, as double for George Kennedy. Later, in **Against A Crooked Sky**, Bjornstad also doubled for Richard Boone.

Dave Sharpe, acknowledged as the greatest daredevil of all, headed the stunt team for **Smoke Signal**. It was rumored that Sharpe belonged to English nobility, but he refused to either confirm or deny the report while on location in southeast Utah. He did, however, speak in the cultured Oxford accent of the upper-class English. Most of his action in **Smoke Signal** took place in flatboats on the Colorado and San Juan rivers. Stuntman Chuck Couch also worked with Sharpe in the action scenes. The movie depicted a lost cavalry patrol's flight from the Indians, using a treacherous river for their getaway. As movie magic goes, they began their flight on the Colorado River and wound up on a rugged stretch of the San Juan.

Moab extras Irma Newell, left, and Essie White, right, pose with a wardrobe man from Hollywood, during filming of **Wagon Master** *in which Essie's dog played a big role. Courtesy of Essie White.*

Horse falls in scene from **Siege at Red River***, at fort built near Locomotive Rock in Professor Valley. Courtesy of Bernice Bowman.*

Smoke Signal Diary

It is interesting to read some of the press releases regarding the movie *Smoke Signal*. One article reported, in part, the following:

The treacherous Colorado River snags the limelight from the stars in the new Universal-International adventure, filmed in and around Moab and on the raging river. In fact, there was almost as much drama behind the camera as before it. There were several near drownings, a boat was wrecked and lost - together with its valuable movie equipment - nine members of the crew suffered water poisoning, director Jerry Hooper was trapped in quicksand, and Piper Laurie suffered a dislocated hip.

Besides these disasters, every member of the cast and crew suffered severe sun- and wind-burn, as well as acute eyestrain, for they had to work on the river between canyon walls more than 1,000 feet high for 30 days in blazing summer temperatures down 200 miles of the Colorado River.

Most of the river scenes were actually filmed on the San Juan River. Clea Johnson of Blanding doubled for Piper Laurie in those scenes. She kept a diary and claims it wasn't quite as bad as the media would have you believe. "There were a few scary moments running the rapids, a few upset stomachs from the water, and a little quicksand is all," says Clea. Excerpts from her diary follow:

First Day: *Left home May 28, 1954 to join Universal-International on the San Juan River trip. When we reached Mexican Hat we immediately got into costumes which we wore for seven days. They loaded the boats and we got on the river. There were eight boats in all, two picture boats, two camera boats, and four equipment boats.*

The boatmen working the picture were Frank Wright, Willard Wright, Don Smith, Duane Bishop, Eugene Bickenstaff, Robert Castleton, Cooney Reppon, Al Codgen, and Kent Frost. Most of the boatmen were put in uniform and some were used in the picture. Willard took the part of Garode, a trapper. Script boy, Bob Forest, did most of the doubling for Dana Andrews. There were twelve film crew, including director Jerry Hopper.

Second Day: *They began shooting pictures. In the head picture boat was Lyle, the double for Captain Harper (William Talman), Bob Forest, double for Halliday (Dana Andrews), Willard (as Garode), Joe Livingston, who played a blind soldier, and myself, in for Piper Laurie. In the second picture boat was boatman Duane Bishop and several movie guys playing soldiers.*

We ate lunch four miles above Government Rapid. I went through my first rapid and they took pictures of us. We camped that night where the road comes in from Clay Hills.

Third Day: *We went on to Piute Farms, where we met Bernal Bradford and a movie executive with supplies and film. Here they shot a scene of the party escaping the Indians. I ducked down in the boat while Captain Harper and Dana Andrews' double got out and began shooting Indians. Men on shore were shooting ball bearings with flippers at us. Livingston (the blind man), wandered out. Halliday went after him and got shot. Halliday gets caught in quicksand, Captain Harper throws a rope and pulls them out, and we escaped the Indians. It was realistic because they really did get in quicksand.*

Fourth Day: *Spent most of the morning getting out of Piute Farms. We had to keep pushing the boats off sand bars. Every time they got ready to take a picture, one of the boats would get stuck. Finally we got down to Piute Rapid. It took hours to get the cameras set up. Lyle and Willard Wright run this rapid. It was the first time it had been run by oars. Then they sent the dummy boat (the vessel carrying dummy actors) through. My dummy lost her head and the boat got pretty well banged up. We camped on the Island between the two rapids and had to ferry across the river.*

Fifth Day: *All interest settled on Piute Rapid. Willard took the camera boat through, then Kent Frost took the other one through. The cameras were bolted to the boats and turned to get pictures of the swirling water. Don Smith took the part of Dana Andrews and tried to rescue a dummy in the rapid. Kent Frost took the rescue boat down. (Found out later that Don was too close to the camera and they could tell who he was, so they couldn't use this shot.)*

We ate lunch just above Syncline Rapid. The picture boat went through with me as Piper Laurie, Lyle as William Talman, Bob as Dana Andrews, Willard as Garode, and two soldiers. We went on the Thirteen Foot Rapid with the camera boat following. Frank took the camera boat through and Willard took the dummy boat. Gwen Smith (a friend who accompanied Clea, since she was the only woman) put on my costume and went down with the picture boat.

Sixth Day: *Shot pictures at Thirteen Foot Rapid. The dummy boat went through and got hung up on a rock. They were rescued by the "submarine" (the boat they were trying to sink for the picture). We got to Hidden Passage and changed clothes. We ate lunch and the movie executives left in the power boat. Everyone was relaxed because the shooting was over. Water fights and lots of fun.*

Seventh Day: *Frank met us in the power boat. We reached Lee's Ferry about 4:00 p.m., and ended a wonderful experience. It was a paid vacation.*

*Piper Laurie's double, Clea Johnson (Blanding), had to rough it during seven-day river run in **Smoke Signal**. Courtesy of Clea Johnson.*

*Burt Reynolds taking a spill at Canyonlands Rodeo Grounds during filming of **Fade In**. Courtesy of The Times-Independent.*

*Battle Scene in movie **Blue** shows stuntman taking a fall into the Colorado river as he is shot from his horse. Courtesy of George White.*

The 1982 galactic adventure film *Spacehunter* brought a whole new dimension to stunt work in the desert. The picture boasted 24 stunt people, all of whom received screen credits. Walter Scott was stunt coordinator, with Ben Dobbins assisting. Jerry Gatlin returned as part of the stunt team, and Greg Walker was stunt double for star Peter Strauss.

This time there were stuntwomen in the group, including Beth Nuffer, Betty Thomas, Ann Chatterton, Joyce McNeal, Lori Scott, and Chere Bryson. In addition to the bevy of stunt people, 11 hang gliding specialists carried out some daring aerial action.

*Working with hang gliders on movie **Spacehunter**, on location near the potash plant. Photo by Tony Osusky.*

In 1984, Chuck Bail, who had experience as both action director and stuntman, directed *Choke Canyon*. Some of the most phenomenal aerial stunts ever filmed were shot in the Moab area for this picture. The movie was dedicated to Richard R. Holley, the aerial coordinator, who was killed in a helicopter crash in California during his next film. Counted among the daring helicopter crew was Darcy Wingo, pilot of the ill-fated *The Twilight Zone* helicopter just three years earlier. In that 1982 incident, actor Vic Morrow and a child extra on the ground were killed.

Choke Canyon, referred to as a "nuclear Western," included heavy artillery attacks, careening off-road chases, and death-defying plane-and-helicopter dogfights. During the course of the aerial dogfight, the script called for a wing walker to stand on top of a biplane, while a large black ball containing nuclear waste dangled beneath the helicopter.

In the air-to-ground action, the biplane touched down on top of a speeding bus loaded with Moab extras, while the helicopter, with its "hot" load, landed in the back of a big truck carrier also racing down the highway. Jim Franklin flew the modified Stearman biplane, while Johnny Cagen did the wing walk. The old state highway that parallels U.S. Interstate-70 near Cisco was used for this sequence. The helicopters were based on the Pete Byrd property, and some of the stunts were performed over his fields.

It was another challenging stunt when the biplane, with wing walker Cagen on top, zoomed under the historic Dewey Bridge, which spans the Colorado River. Residents got a

closer view of the action when the biplane and daring passenger landed on Fourth East in Moab.

In another heart-stopping shot, the helicopter hovered over the canyon off Dead Horse Point while two stuntmen fought up and down the cable that was holding the black ball. This was just too much excitement for most of the spectators on set, many of whom could not bear to watch the daring scene. At no time had the community of Moab witnessed such skill, timing and coordination in stunt work as in *Choke Canyon*. When the movie was released, the New York Times proclaimed, "The chases are dazzling." Jeffrey Lyons of Sneak Previews declared, "The stunts were superb."

Choke Canyon stunts over Dead Horse Point. *Photo by Bego Gerhart.*

Plane on top of bus in **Choke Canyon**. *Photo by Bego Gerhart.*

Biplane zooms up rim at Dead Horse Point with wing walker Johnny Cagen on top, during filming of **Choke Canyon**. *Photo by Bego Gerhart.*

On set of **MacGyver**, *stunt doubles blast off cliff with airplane seat ejection apparatus.*

73

With contemporary movie scenarios came a run of motorcycle and car chases, crashes and explosions, all demanding stunt people. These flicks include: *Easy Rider*, *Electra Glide in Blue*, and *National Lampoon's Vacation*, all with scenes shot in Monument Valley, and *Vanishing Point*, *The Survivalist*, *Nightmare at Noon* and *Thelma and Louise*, filmed around Moab.

In *Nightmare at Noon,* a sensational dogfight was staged between two helicopters, this time over Arches National Park. The scenery in this sequence is nothing less than out-of-this-world.

In the same movie, cars were prepped for a crash and explosion scene on Moab's Center Street. Everything was prepared and stuntmen were ready to roll. A production assistant stationed down the block with his mobile phone thought he heard the order to "roll 'um" - and he did. Wrong! Of three cameras, not a cameraman was at his station. The cars hit, shot into the air, and a fireball rocketed higher than the tree tops. A spectacular stunt - and nothing was on film. Worse yet, the explosion knocked out power and commercial food freezers all over town. The company insurance covered food spoilage, the Moab Film Commission worked at repairing public relations, and the production manager ordered new cars prepped.

The scene was finally captured in one take on the last day of filming, this time with no problems. The crash, the fireball, and the car careened end-over-end, landing only a few feet from the cameraman in the middle of the street. The camera was on the ground, and the operator was flat on his stomach, mesmerized by what was coming at him. The crowd that had gathered to watch the action was frozen in awe. As the mangled wreckage slid to a stop, you could hear a pin drop. Then a little movement and out pops an arm, then a leg, then all of stuntman Bob Miles, unscathed. As his arms went over his head, like a prize fighter who had just won his bout, the crowd cheered. How that man could have emerged, unhurt, out of that totally trashed heap of metal, is a secret only stunt people seem to know.

Many of the stunt greats mentioned in this chapter are featured in the Hollywood Stuntmen's Hall of Fame in Moab, along with the unique paraphernalia used by these courageous and talented people.

Jim Kelly, MFC board member, welcomes John Hagner of Stuntmen's Hall of Fame in a staged fistfight on courthouse steps.

Thelma and Louise *get revenge on an obnoxious trucker. Filmed southeast of Crescent Junction off Highway 191. Photo by Jim Kelly.*

*Scene from 1987 feature, **Nightmare at Noon**. The crash and fiery explosion was filmed in downtown Moab on 200 East Center Street.*

74

Knights, filmed in 1992 throughout Grand and San Juan counties, was another stunt-filled show. Leading lady of the cyborg feature was Kathy Long, a champion kick boxer. Hand-to-hand combat between the cyborgs and the marauders involved some spectacular gymnastics. While Long had a stunt double, Nancy Thurston, she did most of the fight scenes herself. Petite she may be, but Long packs a heck of a wallop in her kick. A bit over-enthusiastic in one scene, her kick packed too much punch when she chopped a stuntman in the throat, sending him to the hospital. Because of the many battles and chases, stuntmen Bobbie Brown, Jon Epstein and Burt Richardson were heavily involved throughout the production.

Photographer for *Knights*, David Emmericks, usually had a "Steadicam" strapped to his body so he could maneuver around the action and capture great footage that would resemble a participants' point of view. (A Steadicam is the trade name for a device that allows the camera operator to keep the camera steady during hand-held shots.)

Kathy Long in fight scene from **Knights**, *with photographer David Emmericks and his Steadicam. Photo by Bego Gerhart.*

Knights is one of several movies that have provided a challenge for local crew people who were rock climbers prior to getting involved with film. These men and women are professionals at hanging a director and cameraman over a cliff, where they can capture a more artsy angle of a specific shot, or at dangling star doubles from high places in super suspense scenes.

Bego Gerhart is one of these skilled climbers and riggers who has also worked as grip and still photographer. He has a special talent for creating any apparatus needed to get the job done. "The more challenging, the better the work," claims Gerhart. He goes on to explain:

Knights was a challenge. We had landing pads over the edges of cliffs for 'airtime' falls. We had a face-first rappel scene with Kathy climbing a huge overhang, while the

camera team was rigged so they wouldn't fall off. We also put the camera up in a tall aspen tree to film cyborgs rapelling down some of the trees.

Actor Kris Kristofferson's double, stuntman Bobbie Brown, somersaults across gap at Pucker Pass overlook, in **Knights**. *Photo by Bego Gerhart.*

Kathy Long's double, Nancy Thurston, in cliff hanging scene for **Knights**. *Photo by Bego Gerhart.*

The 1992 made-for-television movie, **Double Jeopardy**, gave local riggers more challenges. Starring Bruce Boxleitner and Rachel Ward, the picture's rock-climbing scenes were all filmed around Moab.

Rigging with the first unit were locals Dave Lyle, Millie Birdwell, Jay Smith and Dennis Kilker. Kyle Copeland, Monty Risenhoover and Bego Gerhart rigged for second unit, a long 60-foot fall for Rachel Ward's stunt double, Shelly Presson, a world-class sport climber. The dramatic scene had her whizzing off an overhang and dangling midair with her best "dead body" look, reported Gerhart.

*Stuntwoman Shelly Presson dangling from overhang in scene from **Double Jeopardy**. Photo by Bego Gerhart.*

*Cameramen rigged and waiting to capture stunt fall for **Double Jeopardy**. Photo by Bego Gerhart.*

*Rachel Ward (left), star of **Double Jeopardy** and stunt double Shelly Presson. Photo by Bego Gerhart.*

Several 1993 canyon country movies had a Western theme, a scenario heavy with horse falls and dead men plunging off high places. ***Geronimo: An American Legend*** was certainly no exception. In the epic film, cavalry, Indians and Mexican Federales stormed across the red rock desert clashing, retreating and clashing again.

Columbia Pictures brought in scores of "re-enactors" (specialists in re-creating maneuvers of cavalry and others, complete with their own horses and costumes). Allan Graf was stunt coordinator. Don Holyoak, working as a wrangler on the film, was amused when one day he overheard Graf comment: "This movie has stunts that have never been done before." Having worked on some of the old Western classics, Holyoak failed to see any stunts in ***Geronimo*** that he had not seen before. "In fact, there were many old stunts that I didn't see in this picture, simply because they have been outlawed through more stringent enforcement by the Humane Society," Don noted. "I'm sure there were stunts that Graf hadn't seen, because a lot of the old stuff occurred way before his time."

A burro used in ***Geronimo*** had the task of walking across a slickrock area that sloped down to a ten-foot drop, over which he was to slip and fall. Plenty of padding was placed below the drop so the animal would not be injured. The burro was walked back and forth a few times to get accustomed to the routine. The slickrock was then greased and the director called for the cameras to roll. The burro started across, slipped, and over the edge he went, right on cue. The director was not quite happy with the scene and called for a retake. The burro, having wised up the first time, would have *no* part of it. A second burro was brought in and the next run-through worked fine. (The scene was cut during editing.)

Burro, led by actor Matt Damon, going over cliff in Onion Creek.

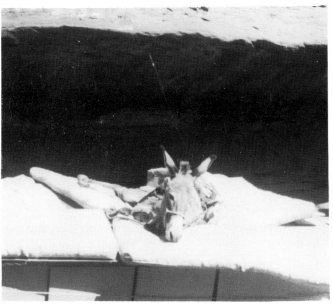

Burro landing on pad and doing fine.

Crew throwing a prosthetic (dummy) burro over cliff in Kane Creek.

*High cliff in Kane Creek, where burro appears to fall over cliff. All burro photos are courtesy of Lynn "Stony" Stones, U.S. Humane Society Officer on the set of **Geronimo**.*

In the movie, viewers would have seen the poor animal falling from a high cliff, and falling and falling. Not to worry. The company moved to another location and threw a dummy burro over the cliff. During editing, the dummy was to have been spliced in where the real burro left off in the fall.

The animals used in movies deserve plenty of credit. The two burros used in **Geronimo** are named Jack and Jill. They belong to head wrangler Rudy Ugland, who furnishes stock for many Western movies. One of his favorite animals is a "fall" horse named Twister. Ugland could never get Twister to do the various tricks most movie horses need to do but, according to Lynn Stones of the Humane Society, Twister finally found his nitch. "He is great at falls," says Stones. "At the tug of the right rein, he jumps, twists in the air, and kicks his feet to the sky as he goes down. He gets restless, just doing chase scenes, but really comes to life when he gets to take a fall."

*Twister, world famous "fall" horse, taking one of his tumbles in chase scene filmed for **Geronimo**. Photo by Lynn Stones.*

*U.S. Humane Officer, Lynn "Stony" Stones, on Twister, during break in filming of **Lightning Jack**, which follwed the production of **Geronimo**. Courtesy of Lynn Stones.*

Hogan's Stunt double David Burton.

*Actor Paul Hogan, star of **Lightning Jack**. Both photos by Lynn Stones.*

SETS AND PROPS

Motion pictures require a few backdrops that nature alone cannot provide. A script may call for an Indian fort, 19th century Western town, Mexican village or a far-out complex on another planet. The art director, working closely with the set designer, is responsible for each set and the overall look of the film. The set designer translates the art director's ideas into a drawing and, when the look is right, drafts construction specifications. The set drawing then takes form and becomes a reality during the preproduction phase of the picture, providing numerous jobs for local contractors and carpenters.

"Props" (short for properties) means any movable items that are seen or used on a film set, but are not structurally parts of the set. Many of the on-location props are brought in by the production company, such as dummy people and horses for the action scenes. Hollywood studios have an enormous variety of props, from custom-made contraptions to the most common items. To meet film demands in Grand and San Juan counties, a number of citizens have collected everything from old skulls, saddles, and tack, to weapons, wagons, and wigwams. When a property call comes down, MMVFC can usually find someone who has the item - or some creative soul who can concoct a facsimile.

Rusty Musselman of Monticello is a "prop master" and worked as a wrangler in many films. He goes way back, and did his share on movies in both Moab and Monument Valley. Over the years Rusty gathered numerous wagons, as well as all kinds of tack and props to have handy for companies when needed. "My dream was to build a Western town, so movie people would have a set when they got here," Rusty recalls. "When the studios stopped making Westerns, I hung on to the stuff for awhile, but eventually sold most of it."

from the rafters and walls. He is still a valuable resource for these types of props. Along with assorted bones and skulls, the general store holds many pieces left over from the big Westerns, silent reminders of the past. Rusty, a crusty old gentlemen with a twinkle in his eye, delights in sharing both his memories and his antiquities with interested passers-by.

During the 1992 filming of *Josh and S.A.M.*, a contemporary feature, nearly all of Rusty's props were used for a set called "Rusty's Reptile Ranch."

Rusty Musselman, long time prop master.

A portion of the set designer's rendition of "Rusty's Reptile Ranch, for movie Josh and S.A.M.

Musselman did get a start on his town. Across from his two-story log home, on a juniper-covered hillside, is the makings of a western street, complete with blacksmith shop, a general store, and other assorted buildings. One structure holds his only remaining wagon, surrounded by all kinds of halters, hames and harnesses, and other leather gear hanging

While the Screen Actors Guild looked after the interests of the stars, the Humane Society was diligent in its concern about the welfare of the animals used in movies. When a scene became too rough for either stuntmen or animals, they were replaced with dummies.

The battle scene in **Blue** is a good example. The Mexican bandits in the movie are ambushed from the banks as they cross the Colorado River. During production, explosives were used as the gang hit the water. After the dust settled, dead horses and bandits could be seen drifting downriver in fast-moving current. When the director called "Cut!" the dummy corpses were quickly retrieved for a retake.

*Prop assistant with a batch of dummy people used in **Blue**. Photo by Lin Ottinger.*

*Battle Scene in the movie **Blue**, as Mexican bandits are ambushed at the river. Photo by Lin Ottinger.*

*Horse dummies being retrieved during filming of **Blue**. Courtesy of George White.*

*A "person" dummy hangs from a truck on **Geronimo** set. Photo by Kari Murphy.*

My Darling Clementine was one of several versions of the Earp Brothers story to appear on film. John Ford, known for his authenticity, had an edge on other directors. According to an account in <u>Arizona Highways</u> (September 1981), Ford knew Wyatt Earp personally. Ford and his wife hosted the famed gunfighter/sheriff in their California home on many occasions. As Earp sipped fine Irish whiskey, he related to the Fords how it really happened at the O.K. Corral. As a result of this firsthand information, Ford had a replica of the town of Tombstone constructed in Monument Valley near Goulding's Lodge. It cost $250,000 for the set, a considerable amount in 1946.

*Actor Henry Fonda relaxes on Tombstone set constructed in Monument Valley for **My Darling Clementine**. The cactus were props brought in to make it look like southern Arizona.*

Film company caravan arriving in Monument Valley on one of the many Westerns filmed there in the forties. Courtesy of The Academy of Motion Picture Arts and Sciences.

The original Gouldings Trading Post and outbuildings, parts of which are shown above, were used as an outpost in **Fort Apache** and **She Wore A Yellow Ribbon**. Photo on right courtesy of The Academy of Motion Picture Arts and Sciences.

*Mexican Village constructed in Professor Valley for movie **Rio Grande**. Photo by Marvin Clever.*

*Army fort at White's Ranch, constructed for **Rio Grande**, and also used for **Battle at Apache Pass** and **Taza, Son of Cochise.** Fort was later dismantled and property is now owned by Colin Fryer. Courtesy of Essie White.*

The Spanish villa for **The Comancheros** *was built near the base of Fisher Towers in Professor Valley. The mansion overlooked a Mexican village (below) in the movie. Head of construction was Al Yubera, who built the famous set at Brownsville, Texas, for* **The Alamo**. *Photo by Marvin Clever.*

On set with **The Comancheros** *near Fisher Towers. Courtesy of Essie White.*

*Set built for **Rio Conchos**, located just north of White's Ranch. Today there is no trace of the set. Photo taken in 1970 by Don Swasey.*

*Scene from **Rio Conchos**, shot in 1964 at the above set. Pictured are actors Stuart Whitman, Richard Boone and Tony Franciosa.*

Set with mansion and distant Indian camp, constructed in Professor Valley near Locomotive Rock for **Rio Conchos**. *Courtesy of George White.*

Scene from **Rio Conchos** *with Edmond O'Brien, as the mansion begins to burn. Photo by Lin Ottinger.*

86

*Fort built for **Smoke Signal** near Locomotive Rock, and later used in **Siege At Red River** for a scene where stars Piper Laurie, Dana Andrews and William Talman escape Indian attack by boat on the nearby Colorado River. Courtesy of George White.*

*Inside the fort, escape boat used in **Siege At Red River** leans against cedar post fencing. Courtesy of George White.*

All that remains of the fort today is this concrete slab put in by Universal International.

*Mexican village constructed west of Klondike Bluffs for the movie **Blue**. Photo by Lin Ottinger.*

*Marvin Clever, builder, working on homestead for **Blue**. Courtesy of Marvin Clever.*

*Homestead for **Blue**, when completed. Set was built near La Sal. Photo by Lin Ottinger.*

Artist rendering of scene from **McKenna's Gold**, *Monument Valley. Courtesy of Academy of Motion Pictures Arts & Sciences.*

Not all movies filmed around Moab and Monument Valley since 1924 have been Westerns or period movies. In 1967, Hollywood finally decided that beautiful scenery and blue skies might also work for a contemporary setting. This meant existing towns and facilities could be used, eliminating the need for much set construction.

When director Silvio Narizzano, producer Jud Bernard, and Bernard's assistant Patricia Casey were scouting for *Blue* near the scenic but isolated Peter Doles cattle ranch in Professor Valley, they conjured up the story of a Moab rancher falling in love with the film editor of the movie *Blue*. Hollywood moves fast. Jerry Ludwig wrote the original screenplay for *Fade In* and, almost overnight, Burt Reynolds was playing his first leading screen role as a Moab rancher. No set construction was necessary, since the key locations became the Dole Ranch and downtown Moab.

In 1968, moviemakers recognized Monument Valley as having galactic possibilities and moved in to film part of *2001: A Space Odyssey*. Southeastern Utah had finally broken the stigma of having been typecast for Westerns only - and barely in time. During the seventies and eighties, the making of Westerns was almost nonexistent.

Moab had its turn depicting outer space with the filming of *Spacehunter*. Jim Foy of Moab constructed the "far-out" sets for this 3-D movie. He later accompanied the crew when they returned to Hollywood to complete the picture.

In addition to the unusual sets developed for this movie, the crew altered the ground surface to make it look more like another planet, then sprayed the bushes in iridescent colors, using water-soluble paint that disappeared with the first rain.

Scene in Woody's Tavern with **Fade In** *stars Barbara Loden and Noam Pittik.*

Spacehunter *set in Long Canyon. Photo by Ron Griffith.*

*Space train built for movie **Spacehunter**, on set near the Texasgulf potash plant, using Rio Grande Railroad rail spur. Courtesy of The Times-Independent.*

*Bizarre sets depict life on the foreign planet Terra 11, in the movie **Spacehunter**. Space land rover is in foreground. Photo by Bego Gerhart.*

Directors today seem as impressed with canyon country as they have always been. But decisions are often based on the geographic area that can furnish two or three "key locations" (sets and locations used most frequently in a picture, or that are most important to the plot).

SMALL TOWN BACKLOTS

It impacts the entire community when a town becomes the key location in a movie. Thompson Springs is a quaint little hamlet northeast of Moab, that frequently gets picked for this reason. Each time it's used, the condensed main street changes entirely.

When director Anthony Hickox selected Thompson Springs as the location for **Sundown: Vampires in Retreat**, the face of the small town was totally changed by the construction of false fronts. Considerable filming was done in the center of town, which is the main entrance to residential areas. Because of roadblocks set up during filming, residents couldn't get to and from their homes and MFC was bombarded with complaints. The production company was asked to limit its road closure times and things quieted down.

The cafe in Thompson Springs was remodeled for **Sundown**. The cafe, which had been closed for years, was improved to such a degree that it reopened after that movie was completed. It remained open for a number of years, and was used again in 1990 for **Thelma and Louise**.

A gas station was constructed for the movie **Sundown** near Hittle Bottom at the north end of Richardson Amphitheater in Professor Valley. One of the scenes called for a stuntman to ride a horse through the front plate-glass window, which was made of sugar and water "candy glass," used in break-through action because it is safer and less expensive than the real thing.

*The "Hemotechnic" plant built in the middle of Thompson Springs for movie **Sundown: Vampires in Retreat**.*

*One of two mansions built at old airport in Spanish Valley for movie **Sundown**. Photo by Larry Nagel.*

*Night shot at gas station built near Hittle Bottom, for 1988 filming of **Sundown**.*

*Cartoon by Moab artist Nik Hougen, who also painted oils to hang in one of the mansions in the **Sundown** movie. Paintings were the mansion itself and of actor David Carradine, who portrayed a vampire.*

*When movie companies come to Thompson Springs, they really jazz up the place. The cafe (to the right) was used in **Sundown**, as well as for **Thelma and Louise**, shown here with a dressed up gas station. The gas station became a jail in **Sundown**.*

Stars Wings Hauser, Bo Hopkins and Kimberly Beck in old Grand County jail for scene in **Nightmare at Noon**.

Dummy doubles for Thelma (actress Geena Davis) left, and Louise (Susan Sarandon) right, were in a T-bird that sailed over a cliff. The Thelma double was retrieved after the crash and has found a home in the Moab-Monument Valley Film and Movie Museum at Red Cliff Lodge.

While filming parts of *Josh and S.A.M.* in 1992, Castle Rock Pictures found it needed a retake of a key location that was filmed in Montana, but didn't want to return to shoot it. They found a Moab home, owned by Joe and Marge Dowd that, with a little set dressing, could double for the previous set. This saved the company considerable expense and Mrs. Dowd was happy to help out.

*On set with **Josh and S.A.M.** at Moab home of Mr. and Mrs. Joe Dowd. Photo by Marge Dowd.*

*The Spanish Valley Trading Post in Moab took on a new look for **Josh and S.A.M.**, after Rusty Musselman provided old bones, horns, and various antiquities.*

In 1992, the filming of *Slaughter of the Innocents* created quite a stir with local environmentalists. Parts of a mock rocky mountain side were built at a gravel pit, off State Highway 128 near the Castle Valley turnoff. The huge structure was then lifted in sections by helicopter and placed on a ledge under the southeast talus slope of Castle Rock, which is on BLM land. The film company also constructed an ark (like Noah's ark) made from about seven tons of materials, and moved it to the same location. The action required that it run along a rail track, which had been built by the crew, and careen over a cliff. The Southern Utah Wilderness Alliance (SUWA), whose members were not happy about the planned project, scheduled their "first annual Lycra Rock Climbing" event on Castle Rock for the same day as the company planned to film the ark scene. (The film permit didn't cover Castle Rock, although it was the major background for the shot.) As it turned out, cold temperatures and stormy weather (and perhaps lack of interest or enthusiasim), caused the climbing event to fizzle.

The inclement weather added to the mysterious atmosphere needed in the film, so the company got its shot - without interference. However, SUWA filed an appeal on the BLM approval of the permit, initiating the action that resulted in more stringent enforcement of BLM policy requiring 45-day permit processing. When the film company wrapped, following the shoot, the area was reclaimed to such a degree that it is difficult to tell that any filming was ever done at the site.

*A rocky mountainside and old mine entrance was built just off State Highway 128, then moved to location for filming of **Slaughter of the Innocents**.*

*The ark built for **Slaughter of the Innocents** and moved to location on a ledge below Castle Rock. In the movie the ark rolls down a track and over the cliff. Courtesy of BLM Grand Resource Area.*

WESTERNS RETURN

Don Holyoak, MFC president, contributed several weeks of complementary guide service during recruitment efforts for the big 1993 **Geronimo** production. Director Walter Hill, while searching for a location to construct Fort San Carlos (a key location), appeared delighted with everything he saw. "Each time we stopped he would say, 'Now this is scenery! Beautiful...breathtaking! But we are not going to do the scene here.' It didn't fit the image in his mind, as it related to the script," reported Holyoak. "When we reached Professor Valley, where the set was finally constructed, Hill felt it had all the qualities for which he had been searching."

When hundreds of thousands of dollars are invested in construction, you can bet film execs will settle for nothing short of the perfect location. This picture required the first major set construction since **Spacehunter** in 1982, and was the first Western filmed in Moab since the mid-Seventies.

Once Columbia Pictures wrapped on **Geronimo: An American Legend**, all sets were taken down and the locations reclaimed, with the exception of one – the Overland Stage Station. This set is located on state land, accessible only through private property belonging to Moab Salt Company. The set was later used in the 1995 western **Cheyenne**, released on TV in 2002.

*Overland stage station constructed near Moab Salt's potash plant for **Geronimo: An American Legend**.*

"Cibecue Creek" Indian village constructed near Moab Salt plant for **Geronimo: An American Legend**.

Old mining camp in **Geronimo** *feature.*

"Fort San Carlos," constructed for **Geronimo** *in Professor Valley, on property owned by Peter Lawson. San Carlos was dismantled following production, and the land reclaimed. Courtesy of Shannon Lavender Rowe.*

Local extra Brody Stevenson, perched on seat of rolling jail, a prop used in **Geronimo**. *Photo by Cindi Stevenson.*

Gene Hackman in front of jail at San Carlos, a set for **Geronimo**.

Set constructed at the Dugout Ranch in San Juan County for **City Slickers II: The Search For Curly's Gold** *was a duplicate of the general store at the Rusty Musselman compound north of Monticello. Musselman furnished most of the props for this set. Photo by Leo Dutilly.*

97

*Small cafe set constructed in Monument Valley for 1993 movie **Pontiac Moon**, starring Ted Danson. Photo by Jeff Beecroft.*

Interior of the cafe. Set materials were later contributed to the Navajo when filming was completed. Photo by Jeff Beecroft.

THE MOVIES

While most Moab-Monument Valley movies made it to the big screen, a few were filmed for television and others wound up on video. Some appear to be lost forever, the victim of decomposing celluloid or buried in a storage vault, too important to save for posterity. This chapter will discuss a few pictures, followed by a complete list of area-filmed movies. Some features were filmed completely in southeastern Utah; others had only segments filmed here. When a director or producer is looking for dramatic and unusual scenery for the opening or ending of a picture, Utah's canyon country is the greatest place on earth.

Indian keeps a silent vigil on bluff in Monument Valley, awaiting white man's intrusion, in **The Vanishing American.**

THE VANISHING AMERICAN (1925) - all dates are when filmed, not necessarily the year of release

LOCATION: Segments filmed in Monument Valley, Utah

CAST: Richard Dix, Lois Wilson, Noah Beery, Malcolm McGregor and Charles Stevens

ABOUT THE MOVIE: Filmed in black-and-white, *The Vanishing American* was the first feature produced in southeastern Utah. Based on a Zane Grey story, the silent movie was about the history of the American Indian and his struggle for survival. It was director George B. Seitz who discovered Monument Valley as a cinema setting, not John Ford as is often believed. Ford did not make his first picture in the land of the monuments until nearly 15 years later.

*Leading lady, Lois Wilson, comforts her hero, Richard Dix, in silent movie **The Vanishing American**.*

*1938 production of **Stagecoach** utilizes the famous Monument Valley vista to show the coach racing over the desert with a "six-up" team of horses. Courtesy of The Academy of Motion Picture Arts and Sciences.*

The Ringo Kid (John Wayne), Buck, the coach driver (Andy Devine), and Sheriff Curly Wilcox (George Bancroft) chat with Francis Ford at stage stop.

STAGECOACH (1938)

LOCATION: Monument Valley (Based at Goulding's Lodge, Utah)

CAST: John Wayne, Claire Trevor, John Carradine, Thomas Mitchell, Andy Devine, Donald Meek, Louise Platt, Tim Holt, George Bancroft, Berton Churchill, Tom Tyler, Chris Pin Martin, Elvira Rios, Francis Ford, Marga Daighton, Kent Odell, Yakima Canutt, Chief Big Tree, Harry Tenbrook, Jack Pennick, Paul McVey, Cornelius Keefe, Florence Lake, Louis Mason, Brenda Flower, Walter McGrail, Joseph Rickson, Vesta Pegg, William Hoffer, Bryant Washburn, Nora Cecil, Helen Gibson, Dorothy Appleby, Buddy Roosevelt, Bill Cody, Chief White Horse, Duke Lee, Mary Kathleen Walker, Ed Brady, Steve Clemente, Theodore Larch, Fritzi Brunette, John Eckert, Al Lee, Jack Mohr, Patsy Dole, Wiggie Blowne, and Margaret Smith

ABOUT THE MOVIE: *Stagecoach* is based on Ernest Haycox's story "Stage to Lordsburg." Director John Ford, a master at conflict and resolution in his films, follows nine people as they confront a spectrum of emotions while making a hazardous journey from the town of Tonto to Lordsburg. Although the travelers are aware of possible Indian trouble, each character has reason for deciding to disregard the danger and take the stagecoach. A feeling of destiny prevails as each individual is faced by fate.

Along the way, Ringo, an escaped outlaw picked up on the trail, falls in love with Dallas, a social outcast because she is considered a "bad" girl. Lucy Mallory, due to advanced pregnancy, is determined to join her husband in Lordsburg. She has the baby en route, at a Mexican outpost. Drunken Doc Boone rises to his professional calling and helps with a successful delivery. Buck, the stage driver, provides the comic relief in the story. Gatewood, the banker, is a highbrow who reminds the others how bad they are and is consistently the "bad guy" in doing so. Peacock, the whiskey drummer, and Hatfield, the gambler, face their own problems. When the group finally reaches its destination, Ringo finds and kills the Plummer brothers who, the viewer has learned, victimized his family and caused him to turn outlaw. In a happy ending, Doc and Curly help Ringo and Dallas make it across the border to safety at Ringo's ranch.

*Wyatt Earp (Henry Fonda) and Clementine Carter (Cathy Downs) pay their last respects to Wyatt's younger brother James, in **My Darling Clementine**.*

Henry Fonda (Wyatt Earp) and Victor Mature (Doc Holliday) prepare for gun fight with the Clayton family at the OK Corral.

MY DARLING CLEMENTINE (1946)

LOCATION: Monument Valley (Based at Goulding's Lodge, Utah)

CAST: Henry Fonda, Linda Darnell, Victor Mature, Walter Brennan, Tim Holt, Ward Bond, Cathy Downs, Alan Mowbray, John Ireland, Grant Withers, Roy Roberts, Jane Darwell, Russell Simpson, Francis Ford, J. Farrell McDonald, Don Garner, Ben Hall, Arthur Walsh, Jack Pennick, Louis Mercier, Micky Simpson, Fred Libby, Harry Woods, Charles Stevens.

ABOUT THE MOVIE: This John Ford movie is based on Stuart N. Lake's novel, "Wyatt Earp, Frontier Marshal." It focuses on the relationship between Wyatt Earp and Doc Holliday.

The movie opens with the Earp brothers driving their cattle west from Texas. Near the town of Tombstone, Arizona, young brother James is left to guard the cattle while the rest head into town. Tombstone is wild and dangerous and Wyatt, after subduing a drunken Indian, is offered the job of town marshal.

Upon returning to camp, the Earp brothers find young James has been murdered and their cattle stolen. Wyatt accepts the job as marshal and begins the hunt for James' killer. The real power in town is Doc Holliday, with whom Wyatt Earp has a confrontation. Arriving at a stalemate, the two become good friends. Clementine Carter, Doc's nurse in the east, comes to Tombstone hoping to persuade "Doc" to go back with her. The marshal takes an interest in Clementine, and Doc becomes increasingly hostile over the attraction between them.

Wyatt suspects the Claytons of rustling his cattle and killing his brother, but his suspicion is turned toward Doc's girlfriend, Chihuahua, when Wyatt finds James's medal in her possession. Immediately after admitting she got the medal from one of the Clayton boys, Chihuahua is shot by Billy Clayton, who had been lurking outside her window. Following an exchange of bullets, Virgil Earp chases the fatally wounded boy back to the Clayton place. Old man Clayton is waiting and kills Virgil.

To settle the affair, the Claytons challenge the remaining Earp brothers at the O.K. Corral. Having lost his love, Chihuahua, Doc Holliday joins the Earps in their battle and meets his end, along with the entire Clayton family. In the final scenes, Wyatt and Morgan Earp take their brothers' bodies home to their father, bidding good-bye to Clementine, who remains in Tombstone.

Three prominent characters in the movie **Fort Apache**, *Lieutenant Colonel Owen Thursday (Henry Fonda), his daughter Philadelphia (Shirley Temple), and Captain Kirby York (John Wayne).*

Captain Kirby York (John Wayne) eulogizing Lieutenant Colonel Thursday (Henry Fonda, in painting) for his heroics during the "Thursday Charge," where Thursday died on the battlefield.

FORT APACHE (1947)

LOCATION: Monument Valley, Mexican Hat, and San Juan River. (Based at Goulding's Lodge, Utah)

CAST: John Wayne, Henry Fonda, Shirley Temple, John Agar, Ward Bond, George O'Brien, Victor McLaglen, Pedro Armendariz, Anna Lee, Irene Rich, Guy Kibbee, Grant Withers, Miguel Inclan, Jack Pennick, Mae Marsh, Dick Moran, Frank Ferguson, Francis Ford, Ray Hyke, Movita Castenada, Mary Gordon.

ABOUT THE MOVIE: Based on James Warner Bellah's story, "Massacre," the feature is another John Ford production. In addition to the conflicts between the cavalry and the Indians, Ford strongly highlights the differences in his lead characters. Lieutenant Colonel Thursday, a staunch military man from the East, takes command of a western outpost, Fort Apache, during a period of Indian trouble with Cochise and his warriors. Thursday is a status-conscious disciplinarian, with no practical sense for dealing with the Indians. His lovely daughter, Philadelphia, has a deep love and respect for her father, but is young and vulnerable and ready for new experiences. Thursday's cold nature surfaces even more in his attitude toward Philadelphia when she falls in love with a West Point graduate, Lieutenant Michael O'Rourke, who has just returned home to Fort Apache.

Captain Kirby York is the direct opposite of Lieutenant Colonel Thursday - relaxed with the ladies, knowledgeable about the Indians, and certainly less rigid with the troops. Captain York persuades Cochise to return to the reservation with his people, telling Cochise that he will be listened to and treated with respect. Concluding the Indians are savages who had broken the treaty by leaving the reservation, Thursday feels no obligation to honor York's word. By the time the inevitable battle is fought, wiping out nearly all the cavalry command, York has learned a degree of discipline from Thursday, making him a better person and leader. Before his death in the onslaught, Thursday's bravery and commitment to his men earn him York's respect. Later, Philadelphia and Michael O'Rourke are married, and York carries out the myth of "Thursday's Charge," for years to come.

*In scene from **Fort Apache**, Lieutenant Colonel Thursday (Henry Fonda) prepares his men for battle. Thursday stands behind Captain Kirby York (John Wayne), kneeling in center.*

SHE WORE A YELLOW RIBBON (1949)

LOCATION: Monument Valley, Mexican Hat, and San Juan River (Based in Utah at Goulding's Lodge)

CAST: John Wayne, Joanne Dru, John Agar, Ben Johnson, Harry Carey, Jr., Victor McLaglen, Mildred Natwick, George O'Brien, Arthur Shields, Francis Ford, Harry Woods, Chief Big Tree, Noble Johnson, Cliff Lyons, Tom Tyler, Michael Dugan, Micky Simpson, Greg Graham, Frank McGrath, Don Summers, Fred Libby, Jack Pennick, Billy Jones, Bill Gettinger, Ford Kennedy, Rudy Bowman, Post Park, Ray Hyke, *Lee Bradley, Chief Sky Eagle, and Dan White. * Local actor

ABOUT THE MOVIE: Based on James Bellah's story, "War Party," this film is another Indian and cavalry picture. It is structured around a lonely army man who is based at a western fort.

Captain Nathan Brittles has lost his wife and daughter and faces imminent military retirement. Following the Little Big Horn, the Indians kill the fort's paymaster and gather for a large attack. The captain is sent on his last mission, which is to find and contain the Indians, thus heading off a war.

Brittles finds himself saddled with two ladies. Miss Olivia Dandridge and her aunt from the East cannot abide life at the fort and decide to leave by stagecoach. The risk to the women prevents the captain from accomplishing his mission, and the Indians, armed for war, wipe out all settlers in their path.

Leaving young Lieutenant Cohill guarding a river crossing, Brittles is forced to return to the fort with the women. Unable to return to help Cohill because his retirement is about to be activated, Brittles is replaced by Lieutenant Pennel. The troops ride off and Brittles cannot restrain himself. He leaves the fort, joins the command, and orders the men to wait while he goes into the Indian camp to try reasoning with the renegades. During his talks with Chief Pony That Walks, the old Indian tells him it is too late, he cannot control his young braves. Red Shirt, leader of the braves, advises Brittles that he can do nothing to stop them.

Waiting until after dark, Brittles and the unit stampede the Indians' horses and a war is thus prevented. Then, his retirement a sudden reality, Brittles departs and rides westward. Sergeant Tyree, a younger version of Brittles, stops him with the news of Brittle's appointment as head of civilian scouts and his new rank as colonel. He joins Tyree and they ride back to the fort.

Chief Pony That Walks (Chief Big Tree) tries to control his young braves and stop the war with white man, during scene from **She Wore A Yellow Ribbon**.

*Indian war party in **She Wore A Yellow Ribbon**. Courtesy of The Academy of Motion Picture Arts and Sciences.*

*Sergeant Tyree (Ben Johnson) spins on his horse to flee Indian attack during scene in **She Wore A Yellow Ribbon**, John Ford's fourth movie filmed in Monument Valley.*

WAGON MASTER (1949)

LOCATION: Professor Valley, Colorado River, and Spanish Valley. (Based in Moab, Utah)

CAST: Ben Johnson, Harry Carey, Jr., Joanne Dru, Ward Bond, Charles Kemper, Alan Mowbray, Jane Darwell, Ruth Clifford, Russell Simpson, James Arness, Fred Libby, Hank Worden, Mickey Simpson, Francis Ford, Cliff Lyons, Don Summers, Movita Castenada, and Jim Thorpe.

ABOUT THE MOVIE: The story recounts the experiences of a westward-bound Mormon (Latter Day Saints) pioneer group, menaced by hostile forces. Two horse traders, Sandy and Travis, meet the Mormon group and Travis is asked to be their wagon master. The wagon train later encounters three itinerant actors in the desert - an older couple and a young woman named Denver - who are lost and near death. In spite of objections from his group, the Mormon elder agrees to take the actors with them until they reach the trail turning off to California.

In addition to the rigors of the journey, the wagon train is threatened by an outlaw family, the Cleggs, who force the Mormons and their wagon master to guide them west. The emotional tension among wagon train members is further charged by the violent and perverse characters of the Cleggs. When the trail fork to California is reached, Travis asks Denver to marry him, but she refuses and the show people depart. The Cleggs, who do not want their location known, go after the actors and bring them back.

The story line shows the interaction of the various groups; the individual characters bring the viewers' own beliefs and moral assumptions to the surface for scrutiny. For instance, the actors' desperate plight in the desert challenges the group complacency and snobbery of the Mormons. Denver's attire and mannerisms require the viewer to see beyond the outward appearance to her potential for change.

When the Cleggs attempt to prevent the Mormons' final crossing to their valley, Sandy and Travis kill the Cleggs. The Mormons, horse traders, and show people are thus united at the end of what, in many ways, may be the high point of John Ford's classic Westerns.

Mormon wagon train is held at gunpoint by the Clegg family in **Wagon Master**.

Travis (Ben Johnson) and Elder Wiggs (Ward Bond) look for a river crossing for the Mormon wagon train, in Wagon Master.

Doctor Locksley Hall (Russell Simpson), with Sister Ledeyard (Jane Darwell) to his left, and Fleuretty Phyffe (Ruth Clifford) to his right, speaks for Mormons during their westward quest, in Wagon Master.

RIO GRANDE (1950)

LOCATIONS: White's Ranch (fort), Ida Gulch, Professor Valley, Colorado River, Onion Creek Narrows. (Based in Moab)

CAST: John Wayne, Maureen O'Hara, Ben Johnson, Claude Jarman, Jr., Harry Carey, Jr., Chill Wills, J. Carroll Naish, Victor McLaglen, Grant Withers, Peter Ortiz, Steve Pendleton, Karalyn Grimes, Albert Morin, Stan Jones, Fred Kennedy, Jack Pennick, Pat Wayne, Chuck Roberson, the Sons of the Pioneers, Ken Curtis, Hugh Farr, Karl Farr, Lloyd Perryman, Shug Fisher, Tommy Doss.

NOTE: Director John Ford had a way of sticking with what he liked. John Wayne played Captain Kirby York (without the "e"), in *Fort Apache*. In *Rio Grande*, Wayne was cast as Lieutenant Colonel Kirby Yorke (with an "e"). Ben Johnson appears again as Tyree. In *She Wore A Yellow Ribbon*, he was a sergeant and in *Rio Grande* he played a trooper.

*Lieutenant Colonel Kirby Yorke (John Wayne) leads his men into Fort Stark, in scene from **Rio Grande**. Courtesy of Essie White.*

ABOUT THE MOVIE: Colonel Kirby Yorke, commanding officer at Fort Stark, has been frustrated in his efforts to pacify the Apaches because the government will not permit him to follow them across the Rio Grande River into Mexico. Yorke's son, whom he has not seen in 15 years, has just flunked out of West Point and joined the Army as an enlisted man. His first assignment is to his father's command. The young trooper is put through the usual initiation rites - challenges in horsemanship and camp fighting - while his father watches from the sidelines.

Colonel Yorke is subsequently joined by his estranged wife, whom he also has not seen in 15 years. She followed their son to Fort Stark to get him to resign from the army. "Ramrod, wreckage and ruin" are Mrs. Yorke's views of her husband and the Army, views tempered only by her enjoyment of the regimental singers, played by the Sons of the Pioneers.

Apache Chief Natchez and part of his band are being held prisoner at the fort. After others of Natchez' warriors free the captives, Yorke's regiment must take to the field to recapture them. An unsuccessful pursuit occurs, which is again stopped at the Rio Grande. This failure ultimately leads to an "unofficial" order to Colonel Yorke to stop the Indians once and for all by crossing the Rio Grande, if necessary.

In preparation for this campaign, the women (including Mrs. Yorke) and children are to be evacuated to the safety of Fort Bliss, with an escort that includes Trooper Yorke. While en route, the party is attacked and several of the women and children are kidnaped. The rescue effort is heroically aided by the daring efforts of Trooper Yorke but marred by the wounding of his father at the end of the successful battle. Both are subsequently welcomed home as heroes by Mrs. Yorke, and a family reconciliation follows.

*Scene in **Rio Grande**. U.S. Cavalry charges Mexican village where Indians are holding children hostage. Courtesy of George White.*

112

Indians prepare for ambush at Apache Pass (actually filmed at Arches National Monument) in **Battle At Apache Pass**. *Courtesy of The Academy of Motion Picture Arts and Sciences.*

BATTLE AT APACHE PASS (1952)

LOCATIONS: Sand Flats, Courthouse Wash, Arches National Monument (now Park), Professor Valley, Ida Gulch, Colorado River (Based in Moab)

CAST: Jeff Chandler, John Lund, Susan Cabot, Beverly Tyler, Jay Silverheels, Richard Egan, Bruce Cowling, James Best, Tommy Cook, Regis Toomey, Jack Elam, Richard Garland, Jack Ingram, Hugh O'Brian, Gregg Palmer, *Lee Bradley, William Reynolds. *Local actor

NOTE: The role of Cochise was played by Jeff Chandler, who was nominated for an Academy Award for the same role in **Broken Arrow** two years earlier.

ABOUT THE MOVIE: **Battle At Apache Pass** is the first movie made in technicolor on location in Moab. In the story, two Chiricahua Apache chiefs, Cochise and Geronimo, face each other in a bitter personal feud. Major Colton, in command of an outpost in southern Arizona, is a trusted friend of Cochise.

Lieutenant Bascom, fresh from West Point and trying to make a name for himself, incites Cochise to go against the "white eyes." When a small boy is kidnaped by Indians, Cochise is wrongly blamed. When the Apache chief denies possessing the boy, Lt. Bascom strings up several Indian hostages to the nearest tree. Later, it is proven that Coyotero Apaches abducted the youngster.

Years later the same lad shows up again, known as Mickey Free, an unscrupulous, hot-tempered "squaw man," married to an Apache girl. He scouts for the American Army in its search for Geronimo, who has been raiding with fury. The climactic battle scene at Apache Pass in the Chiricahua Mountains pits the Apache tribes against the U.S. Cavalry. The Indians have little chance against the cavalry's artillery.

NOTE: Much has been said about the myths of the classic Westerns. While in Moab, director George Sherman revealed how he had taken full advantage of "poetic license" with the screenplay for **Battle At Apache Pass**. He insisted that historical alterations were done because Hollywood aims to provide entertainment, not museum pieces. He gave the following examples:

1. Cochise and Geronimo face each other in a bitter feud.

FACT: Cochise headed the Chiricahua Tribe of the Apache Nation under warrior Mangas Colorado in 1863. Geronimo was too young to lead anything at that time except games among his playmates. He didn't begin his blood-spilling tactics until almost 20 years later.

2. In the movie, Cochise has only one wife, Nona, and Geronimo is unmarried.

FACT: Cochise had four wives and Geronimo had seven. (Sherman noted it is hard to develop a real love story if a man has several wives).

3. A deep love was shown between Cochise and Nona.

FACT: According to history, Apache men appeared to have little use for their women.

4. Major Colton was a trusted friend of Cochise.

FACT: The only army officer the Apache chief ever trusted was General Howard.

Cochise (Jeff Chandler) has talk with fellow Apaches in **Battle At Apache Pass**. *Courtesy of The Academy of Motion Picture Arts and Sciences.*

114

The U.S. Cavalry prepares to march into a canyon where Apaches wait in ambush in **Taza, Son of Cochise**, *sequel to* **Battle At Apache Pass**. *Courtesy of George White.*

115

Taza (Rock Hudson), on a peace mission, talks with officers at the fort during scene from **Taza, Son of Cochise***. Courtesy of George White.*

TAZA, SON OF COCHISE (1953)

LOCATIONS: White's Ranch (fort), Castle Valley, Professor Valley, Sand Flats (Based in Moab)

CAST: Rock Hudson, Jeff Chandler, Barbara Rush, Bart Roberts, Gregg Palmer, Ian MacDonald, Morris Ankrum, Joe Sawyer, Robert Burton, Lance Fuller, Brad Jackson, Richard Cutting, Gene Iglesias, *Barbara Burck, John Day, Charles Horvath, Jack Williams, Bobby Hoy, Al Wyatt, Joe Yrigoyen, James Van Horn. * Local actress

ABOUT THE MOVIE: Filmed in 3-D technicolor with stereophonic sound, **Taza, Son of Cochise** is a sequel to **Battle At Apache Pass**. In this story, Cochise dies and hands over tribal leadership to his son, Taza. Peace-loving Taza tries not to be influenced by Geronimo, as he steps forward to assume leadership over the Apache domain. At the same time, a beautiful romance develops between Taza and an Apache beauty, Oona.

    Geronimo leads his warriors on the warpath, raiding and killing white settlers. The picture is action-packed, with fighting among the Indians, as well as raids on the fort, wagon train and settlers. Taza is finally able to gain control and develop some semblance of order in the great Southwest.

116

*Renegade Indians burn wagon after killing the occupants during a dramatic attack in movie, **Taza, Son of Cochise**. Courtesy of The Times-Independent.*

Taza (Rock Hudson) working with the U.S. Cavalry for peace, tries to explain the plan to fellow Apaches.

Major Indian attack on fort, the final sequence in **Siege At Red River**. *Courtesy of George White.*

SIEGE AT RED RIVER (1953)

LOCATIONS: Locomotive Rock, Colorado River, Castle Valley, Professor Valley (Based in Moab)

CAST: Van Johnson, Joanne Dru, Richard Boone, Milburn Stone, Jeff Morrow, and Craig Hill.

ABOUT THE MOVIE: The working title of this technicolor picture was *Gatling Gun*. This name provides a clue to part of the story, which takes place during the American Civil War.

A confederate agent, operating behind northern lines, is betrayed by a treacherous assistant and manages to escape to the South. Intrigue, action and romance in the movie are presented in such a way that it is acceptable for viewing by the entire family. The movie ends with a major Indian attack on the fort, where troops have managed to acquire a gatling gun. The Indians are no match for this rapid-firing weapon and the fort is saved.

NOTE: To make the background more believable as somewhere in the Southeast, some shots were filmed in Durango, Colorado, where there is less desert country.

SMOKE SIGNAL (1954)

LOCATIONS: "Big Bend" of the Colorado River, Professor Valley, Ida Gulch, Colorado River, Mexican Hat, and the San Juan River (Based at Moab)

CAST: Dana Andrews, Piper Laurie, Rex Reason, William Talman, Douglas Spencer, Milburn Stone, William Schallert, Bill Phipps, Bob Willke, Gordon Jones, Pat Hogan, and Peter Coe.

      NOTE: Bart Roberts in *Taza, Son of Cochise* is the same actor known as Rex Reason in *Smoke Signal*. Christened Rex Reason at birth and given Roberts by Hollywood, the actor later returned to using his real name.

ABOUT THE MOVIE: Filmed in black-and-white, *Smoke Signal* is one of the few "river-running" Westerns ever filmed. Surviving an Indian massacre at the fort, a lost cavalry patrol takes to the river in flatboats to escape the Indians. A renegade soldier of fortune, wanted for desertion from the U.S. Army, leads them in their flight to safety.

      A romantic triangle develops between a lone girl in the group, the renegade soldier, and another trooper. In the course of their journey, tension builds and the men battle among themselves. Eventually, the trooper tries to kill the leader, but falls headlong off a canyon rim to his death. Indians and personal differences become secondary to the danger of the roaring whitewater rapids that confront them farther downriver. Upon bringing the group through safely, the renegade soldier becomes a hero, winning the girl and respect from all.

*In **Smoke Signal**, renegade soldier and deserter (Dana Andrews) held at gunpoint by trooper (William Talman) as others look on, including the lone female in the picture, Piper Laurie. The group is escaping an Indian attack down the dangerous Colorado River.*

CANYON CROSSROADS (1954)

LOCATIONS: Moab City, Professor Valley, and Sevenmile Canyon (Based in Moab)

CAST: Richard Basehart, Phyllis Kirk, Stephen Elliott, Russell Collins, and Charles Wagenheim

ABOUT THE MOVIE: Filmed in black-and-white by an independent New York company, *Canyon Crossroads* is a modern-day Western. The story of a prospector's search for space-age ore, the movie was inspired by the famed Mi Vida uranium strike made by Moab's own Charles Steen. Producers used actual Moab area mines, along with technical knowledge and equipment of the day, while filming this documentary style movie. The prospector in the film is trailed by thieves, resulting in a showdown. The prospector (good guy) of course comes out the winner.

Prospectors (Phyllis Kirk, Richard Basehart, and Russell Collins) in their search for uranium during scene in **Canyon Crossroads***.*

*Martin Pawley (Jeffrey Hunter), Ethan Edwards (John Wayne) and Brad Jorgensen (Harry Carey, Jr.) as they track Comanches who killed one of Ethan's nieces and hold another one captive, in **The Searchers**.*

THE SEARCHERS (1955)

LOCATIONS: Monument Valley and Mexican Hat, Utah (Based at Goulding's Lodge, Utah)

CAST: John Wayne, Jeffrey Hunter, Vera Miles, Ward Bond, Natalie Wood, John Qualen, Olive Carey, Henry Brandon, Ken Curtis, Harry Carey, Jr., Antonio Moreno, Hank Worden, Lana Wood, Walter Coy, Dorothy Jordan, Pippa Scott, Pat Wayne, Beulah Archuletta, Jack Pennick, Peter Mamokos, Cliff Lyons, Billy Cartledge, Chuck Hayward, Slim Hightower, Fred Kennedy, Frank McGrath, Chuck Roberson, Dale Van Sickle, Henry Wills, *Terry Wilson, *Away Luna, *Billy Yellow, *Bob Many Mules, *Exactly Sonnie Betsuie, *Feather Hat, Jr., *Harry Black Horse, *Jack Tin Horn, *Many Mules Son, *Percy Shooting Star, *Pete Grey Eyes, *Pipe Line Begishe, *Smile White Sheep, Mae Marsh, Dan Borzage.   * Local Native American actors

ABOUT THE MOVIE: *The Searchers* is another John Ford Western, this one based on an Alan Le May novel. Ethan Edwards, oldest brother in the family, has just returned home after the Civil War. A Texas Ranger arrives to ask for volunteers to track rustlers. Ethan joins them, as does Martin Pauley, a part-Cherokee boy found by Ethan and adopted by his brother's family. The volunteer posse finds the cattle slaughtered, the result of a Comanche raid.

When Ethan and Martin return to the ranch, they find it burned and the family murdered, with the exception of Ethan's nieces, Debbie and Lucy. It is presumed the girls have been taken captive by Comanches, and the search begins. Ethan and Martin are joined by Brad Jorgensen, who has a personal interest in Lucy, the older girl.

Lucy is soon found dead. Crazed with grief, Jorgensen charges an Indian encampment and is immediately killed. For the next five years, Ethan and Martin continue their search for Debbie. By the time the right Comanche band is located, Debbie has already been taken as wife by the leader, Scar. Wounded in an attempt to rescue Debbie, Ethan leaves, bitter because he feels that Debbie has been too soiled to ever return to white man's society.

Scar's band eventually camps near where Ethan is staying. Martin, afraid Ethan intends to kill Debbie, goes into the Indian camp after her. He manages to kill Scar and escapes with the girl. Ethan rides in and scalps Scar, then goes after Debbie. Catching her, Ethan fights conflicting emotions for one suspense-filled moment, then lifts her in his arms and carries her home.

*In **The Searchers**, Ethan (John Wayne) and Martin (Jeffrey Hunter) rescue Debbie (Natalie Wood) after she has been held captive by the Comanches for many years.*

*Johnie Ganan (Richard Widmark), gunman-turned-sheriff in movie **Warlock**. Courtesy of George White.*

*Lily (Dorothy Malone), in a graveside scene from **Warlock**. Courtesy of George White.*

WARLOCK (1958)

LOCATIONS: Professor Valley, Dead Horse Point, Dole/Bates Ranch, King's Bottom, Arches National Monument, and Sand Flats (Based in Moab) **NOTE:** The outdoor scenes and "San Pablo" were filmed near Moab. The town of "Warlock" was a California set.

CAST: Richard Widmark, Henry Fonda, Anthony Quinn, Dorothy Malone, Dolores Michaels, Wallace Ford, Tom Drake, Richard Arlen, Regis Toomey, Don Beddoe, and De Forest Kelley.

ABOUT THE MOVIE: A DeLuxe Cinemascope picture, this story is about the small western town of Warlock, where the citizens are terrified by a band of cowboy-outlaws from the San Pablo cattle outfit. The sheriff is run out of town and the cowardly citizens hire a gunman, Clay Blaisdell, as their unofficial marshal.

Blaisdell has a long-time sidekick named Tom Morgan, a crippled gambler with a lust for violence. He is highly protective of Blaisdell. A stagecoach is held up by some of the San Pablo boys and Lily, another old acquaintance of Morgan and Blaisdell, is on board. She and her companion, Bob Nicholson, are en route to kill Blaisdell. Morgan watches the robbery from the sidelines and shoots Nicholson. The cowboys are blamed for the murder. A reformed San Pablo bandit, Johnie Ganan, is officially sworn in as Warlock's deputy sheriff, which ultimately leads to a confrontation with his old outfit. The frightened citizens find courage to support Ganan and take back their town. Romantic interest develops between Lily and Ganan.

SERGEANT RUTLEDGE (1959)

LOCATIONS: Monument Valley and Mexican Hat (Based at Goulding's Lodge, Utah)

CAST: Jeffrey Hunter, Constance Towers, Woody Strode, Billie Burke, Juano Hernandez, Willis Bouchey, Carleton Young, Judson Pratt, Bill Henry, Walter Reed, Chuck Hayward, Fred Libby, Toby Richards, Jan Styne, Cliff Lyons, Charles Seel, Jack Pennick, Hank Worden, Chuck Roberson, Eva Novak, Estelle Winwood, and Shug Fisher.
NOTE: This was the only picture where John Ford cast a black man as a hero.

ABOUT THE MOVIE: Filmed in black-and-white, the working titles were *The Trial of Sergeant Rutledge* and *Captain Buffalo*.

The story, set in 1881, is about a black army sergeant in the Ninth Cavalry who is wrongfully charged with rape and murder. Lucy Dabney, the sergeant's friend, is found raped and strangled and her father murdered. Rutledge, away from his post at the time of the heinous crime, is presumed responsible.

Lieutenant Tom Cantrell, also from the Ninth Cavalry, defends Rutledge, and the story unfolds through a series of flashbacks, as told in the courtroom. The movie flashes back to Cantrell's first meeting with Mary Beecher, who provides a love interest. She gets off a train at Spindle Station, where she is to meet her father, only to find that the Apaches have jumped the reservation and killed the station master. Rutledge, who was at the station and was wounded in the attack, protects Mary from the Indians.

The next morning, Cantrell and his men come to arrest Rutledge. While taking Rutledge in, Cantrell and his troops are attacked by Indians and the sergeant escapes. When he sees that the Ninth Cavalry is riding into an ambush, however, Rutledge returns and saves them. Although reluctant, Cantrell knows his duty is to bring the black man in for trial.

In a racist white man's court, Rutledge is badgered by the prosecution, but makes clear his devotion to the Ninth Cavalry. Cantrell eventually uncovers the real murderer and Rutledge is cleared.

Lieutenant Tom Cantrell (Jeffrey Hunter) and Marcy Beecher (Constance Towers) during one of their closer moments in **Sergeant Rutledge.**

*Three cowboys (Clint Walker, Chill Wills, and Roger Moore), as they are confronted by bandits who are after the gold they are carrying, in scene from **Gold of the Seven Saints**.*

GOLD OF THE SEVEN SAINTS (1960)

LOCATIONS: Fisher Towers, Colorado River, White's Ranch, Arches National Monument, Dead Horse Point, Sevenmile Wash, and Klondike Flats (Based in Moab)

CAST: Clint Walker, Roger Moore, Chill Wills, Leticia Moman, Robert Middleton, Gene Evans, Bob Henderson, and Jack Willis.

ABOUT THE MOVIE: This first picture made by Warner Brothers in Moab was filmed in black-and-white Warnerscope. The story involves three cowboys and their search for lost gold. Once the treasure is found, they try to get it across the Rio Grande River to the city of Seven Saints. Some dissension develops among the men as they make their quest southward.

A group of Mexican bandits attacks their camp, causing the treasure hunters' problems to seem less severe. Following a shoot-out, the bandits continue to trail the cowboys, suspecting that they have the gold. When they reach the Rio Grande, the bandits attack again, and the boys lose the stash in the river. After seeing their empty saddlebags, the bandits depart. The gold bars are later recovered and the cowboy's mission is finally accomplished.

THE COMANCHEROS (1961)

LOCATIONS: Professor Valley, Dead Horse Point, King's Bottom, Fisher Valley, Onion Creek, and La Sal Mountains (Based at Moab)

CAST: John Wayne, Stuart Whitman, Ina Balin, Bruce Cabot, Lee Marvin, Edgar Buchanan, Patrick Wayne, and Nehemiah Persoff.

ABOUT THE MOVIE: *The Comancheros* is a highly spirited Western filmed in DeLuxe Cinemascope and directed by George Sherman. In the story, a Texas Ranger is bringing in prisoner Paul Regret, who had killed a man in a duel. At the same time, the ranger is trying to recover rifles being smuggled to a Comanchero compound. The Comancheros are a highly structured group of cowboys, outlaws, Mexicans and Indians who raid pioneer homesteads, stealing cattle and killing anyone who gets in their way. Under the alias of Ed McBain, the ranger meets gunrunner Tully Crowe, who has the rifles. McBain eventually kills Crowe in a poker game.

After removing the firing pins, McBain and Regret deliver a wagon load of rifles to the Comanchero camp. Pilar, daughter of the Comanchero leader, is attracted to Regret. McBain and Regret, aided by Pilar, escape from the Comanchero compound, but are soon surrounded by the well-armed and mounted Comancheros.

In the nick of time, the Texas Rangers arrive and make short work of the Comancheros. McBain rides away with the rangers, bidding a fond farewell to Regret and Pilar.

Texas Ranger Ed McBain (John Wayne) and prisoner Paul Regret (Stuart Whitman) are attacked by Indians in scene from **The Comancheros***. Courtesy of The Academy of Motion Picture Arts and Sciences.*

Deborah Wright (Carroll Baker), Quaker woman who teaches the Indian children, listens to Dull Knife (Gilbert Roland), as Dolores Del Rio looks on. The scene is from the movie **Cheyenne Autumn**, *filmed in both Moab and Monument Valley.*

CHEYENNE AUTUMN (1963)

LOCATIONS: White's Ranch, Castle Valley, Professor Valley, Colorado River, Onion Creek, Arches National Monument, Monument Valley, and Mexican Hat, Utah (Based at Moab and Monument Valley)

CAST: Richard Widmark, Carroll Baker, James Stewart, Edward G. Robinson, Karl Malden, Sal Mineo, Dolores Del Rio, Ricardo Montalban, Gilbert Roland, Arthur Kennedy, Patrick Wayne, Elizabeth Allen, John Carradine, Victor Jory, Mike Mazurki, George O'Brien, Sean McClory, Judson Pratt, Carmen D'Antonio, Ken Curtis, Walter Baldwin, Shug Fisher, Nancy Hsueh, Chuck Roberson, Harry Carey, Jr., Ben Johnson, Jimmy O'Hara, Chuck Hayward, *Lee Bradley, *Frank Bradley, Walter Reed, Willis Bouchey, Carleton Young, Denver Pyle, John Qualen, Nanomba "Moonbeam" Morten, Dan Borzage, Dean Smith, David H. Miller, Bing Russell. **NOTE:** Many well-known actors played very minor roles in this film, probably more than in any other Western. *Local actors

ABOUT THE MOVIE: Based on Mari Sandoy's novel, the movie represents director John Ford's attempt to show the Indian point of view in American history. This technicolor feature is set in the 1860s.

The story is about the Cheyenne Indians who were forced to move to a new reservation 1,500 miles from their ancestral land. Once there, they are guarded by the U.S. Government, which fails to provide sufficient food and shelter for their survival.

Many of the Cheyenne people die from starvation and disease. They then decide to return to their homeland in spite of the government. They are joined by Deborah Wright, a Quaker woman, who teaches the Indian children. Departing in the middle of the night, they are pursued by the U.S. Cavalry, led by Captain Thomas Archer.

Forced into constant skirmishes with the cavalry, the Cheyenne continue their trek homeward. Confronted by hunger, cold, cavalry and the settlers whose land they are crossing, they eventually split into two groups. One group follows Dull Knife to Fort Robins where they hope to get food and shelter for the winter, and the other goes with Little Wolf, continuing their journey to the Cheyenne Nation.

At Fort Robins the Indians are locked up and starved, under orders from a Prussian commander, Captain Wessels, unless they agree to return to the government reservation. They refuse, and many are killed in an escape attempt.

Captain Archer takes up the Cheyenne cause and travels to Washington, D.C. to plead their case. The Secretary of the Interior finally agrees with Archer and allows the few remaining Indians to return to the land of their ancestors.

U.S. Cavalry readies to head off the escaping Cheyenne, who are trying to get back to their homeland, in movie **Cheyenne Autumn***.*

Little Wolf (Ricardo Montalban) and Dull Knife (Gilbert Roland) discuss splitting the Cheyenne Tribe, with some continuing homeward and others seeking shelter for the winter. Red Shirt (Sal Mineo), a spirited young brave, has his own ideas.

RIO CONCHOS (1964)

LOCATIONS: White's Ranch, Castle Valley, Professor Valley, Locomotive Rock, Arches National Monument, and Dead Horse Point State Park (Based in Moab)

CAST: Richard Boone, Stuart Whitman, Tony Franciosa, Jim Brown (professional football player), Wende Wagner, Edmond O'Brien, Rodolfo Acasta, Barry Kelly, Veto Scolie, Kevin Hogen, Haus Peters, Jr., and Warner Anderson.

ABOUT THE MOVIE: *Rio Conchos* is an adventure filmed in Deluxe Cimemascope and set in the post-Civil War era of the West. A military shipment of Spencer rifles has been stolen, and U.S. Cavalry Captain Haven, from whom it was originally taken, has been assigned to recover the rifles. On this mission he is accompanied by an ex-Confederate major named Lassiter, who is an alcoholic and confirmed Indian-hater. Also with him are U.S. Cavalry Sergeant Franklin and a convicted murderer named Rodriguez, whom Lassiter reprieves from the gallows in exchange for the convict's cooperation.

Lassiter learns that his former commander, General Pardee, who has delusions of imperialistic grandeur, has the rifles, which he intends to trade to the Apaches for gold and silver to finance a continuation of the war against the North. Captain Haven and his small group set out to find Pardee. They carry a wagonload of gunpowder to use as bait or, if necessary, to destroy the rifles, should they be unable to retrieve them. Before going very far, Haven's group encounters a silent and hostile Indian girl whom they add to their party. It is hoped that she will eventually agree to lead them to the location where the exchange between the Apaches and Pardee is to take place. In their search for Pardee, they are waylaid by banditos in Mexico, become temporary custodians of a baby whose mother has been killed by the Indians, and are obstructed by Texas Rangers, Mother Nature, and the treachery of Rodriguez.

The group survives all these trials and Pardee is eventually located. Haven, Lassiter, and Franklin are captured and tortured by Pardee's Apaches, but are freed by the silent Apache girl who has fallen in love with Captain Haven. Lassiter and Franklin manage to destroy the rifles, as well as Pardee's dreams for an evil empire. Lassiter and Franklin, alas, sacrifice themselves in the process, and in the final scene Haven and the girl slip away together.

Sergeant Franklin (Jim Brown) is trying to free Lassiter (Richard Boone), who is being held captive at Pardee's mansion in the desert. Courtesy of The Times-Independent.

130

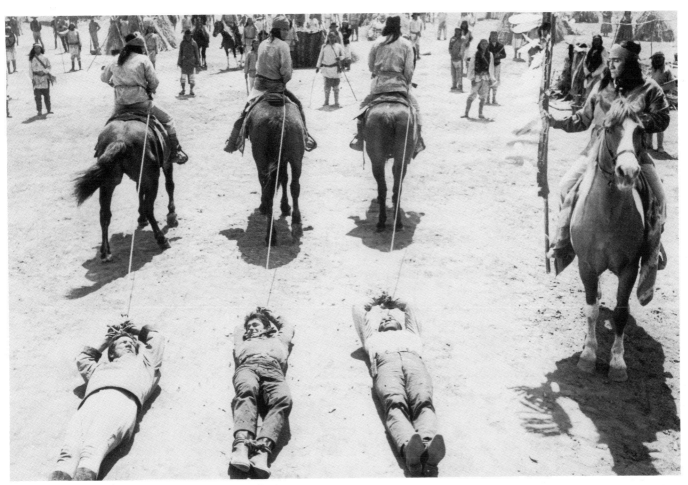

*In scene from **Rio Conchos**, Lassiter (Richard Boone), Captain Haven (Stuart Whitman), and Sergeant Franklin (Jim Brown) are dragged through an Indian camp.*

*Frank Post (William Holden) drives buckboard with cowboy Ross Bodine (Ryan O'Neal), in scene from **Wild Rovers**.*

131

WILD ROVERS (1966 - not released until 1971)

LOCATIONS: Arches National Park and Monument Valley (Based at Moab and Monument Valley)

CAST: William Holden, Ryan O'Neal, Karl Malden, Lynn Carlin, Tom Skerritt, Joe Don Baker, Rachel Roberts, Leora Dana, and Moses Gunn.

ABOUT THE MOVIE: Filmed in Metrocolor Panavision, the story centers on a middle-aged cowboy named Post, who is depressed with his state of life. Post meets Bodine, a younger man, and decides to join him in robbing a bank.

Bodine is wounded in the course of their getaway following the robbery. When the wound begins to trouble him and he can no longer ride, Post rigs up a travois to transport him. They stop to rest and Post begins to describe the life they are heading for in Mexico. Bodine quietly dies. Director Blake Edwards manages a balance of drama and comedy in this rather unusual Western.

Post (William Holden) in scene for **Wild Rovers**, *shot in Monument Valley.*

*In scene from **Blue**, Angel Ortega (Ricardo Montalban) hands wanted poster to adopted son Blue (Terence Stamp), as real son, Costillo Ortega (Carlos East), looks on.*

BLUE (1967)

LOCATIONS: Professor Valley, Colorado River, Sevenmile Canyon, Sand Flats, La Sal, Redd's Ranch, and Wood's Ranch. (Based in Moab)

CAST: Terence Stamp, Karl Malden, Joanna Pettet, Ricardo Montalban, Carlos East, Joe De Santis, Stathis Giallelis, Anthony Costello, James Westerfield, Robert Lipton, Kevin Corcoran, Sara Vardi, Peggy Lipton, Michael Bell, Michael Maxim-Nader, *Shawn Knutson, *Ivalou Redd, Marlyn Mason, Carmen D'Antonio, Irina Marquez, Jane Hoag, Helen Kleeb, Jerry Gatlin, Harold Hickman*, Sally Kirkland, Len Felber, Dorothy Conrad, Dick Farnsworth, Wes Bishop, Ron Masters, Virginia Ellis, Bill Benson, Gary McLarty, Billy Shannon, Walt LaRue, Alma Beltrand, Gary Combs, Buff Brady, LeRoy Johnson, Everett Creach, and Jim Shepard. * Local actors

ABOUT THE MOVIE: Filmed in Technicolor Panavision, the story concerns a white boy, "Blue" Azul, who has been adopted by the Mexican bandit chieftain, Angel Ortega. While on a raid in a Texas border town, Blue prevents his cohorts from raping a white girl and soon falls in love with her. She is the daughter of a prominent citizen, called Doc. Costillo, Ortega's real son, has also lost his heart to Doc's daughter, but becomes the rejected suitor after Blue rescues the girl.

Angel Ortega is a proud man on the verge of destruction as he hopes for a return to his glory days. Blue, a rough-edged bandito, struggles between his heritages; does he want to be a bandit or lead a respectable life?

In a final battle between the town and the Mexican bandits, Blue loses his life but saves Doc's daughter. Ortega realizes his way of life is over and a new age will dawn.

*Doc (Karl Malden) with daughter (Joanna Pettet) in scene from **Blue**.*

In scene at Mexican village, Angel Ortega (Ricardo Montalban) rides out of the cantina with a "lady of the night" over his saddle.

*Moab rancher (Burt Reynolds) and screen editor (Barbara Loden) work on film edits for movie **Blue**, in feature **Fade In**.*

FADE IN (1967)

LOCATIONS: Moab City: Holiday Theater, Woody's Bar, Miller's Shopping Center, and Millcreek bridge on Main Street; also Canyonlands Rodeo Grounds, Dole Ranch, Colorado River, Fisher Towers, and occasional fade-ins to the locations of the movie **Blue**. (Based in Moab)

CAST: Burt Reynolds, Barbara Loden, Patricia Casey, Noam Pitlik, James Hampton, Lawrence Heller, Joseph Perry, and Steve Ferry.

ABOUT THE MOVIE: *Fade In* deals with a Moab rancher falling for the Hollywood film editor who is in town for the production of the movie **Blue**. The inspiration for this scenario came about when film officials were in Moab checking locations for the movie **Blue**, and ordered a script drafted accordingly.

In *Fade In*, the rancher and his happy-go-lucky sidekick, Bud, apply for work in the movie **Blue**. The rancher soon finds himself attracted to the film editor. While the feeling is mutual, she has developed a friendship with the camera operator, who holds the beer drinking record at Woody's Bar. A number of clashes occur as Hollywood crew people mix with the locals, resulting in fistfights, car chases, and other rough-and-tumble action.

The romance between the rancher and film editor flourishes, then suddenly the production of **Blue** is completed and the fairy tale must come to an end. The lovers conclude that the differences between their lives are too great for their relationship to survive. She flies back to Hollywood and he has an experience to remember.

*Burt Reynolds, portraying Moab rancher, rides his range in **Fade In**, on location near Fisher Towers. Photo by Lin Ottinger.*

EASY RIDER (1968)

LOCATIONS: Segments filmed in Monument Valley

CAST: Peter Fonda, Jack Nicholson, Dennis Hopper, Launa Anderson, Robert Walker, and Karen Black.

ABOUT THE MOVIE: The story, filmed in Technicolor, involves two society dropouts who decide to ride across America on motorcycles. *Easy Rider* is an unusual melodrama, with a little sprinkling of politics and philosophy mixed with adventure, as the motorcycle enthusiasts continue their quest of "searching for America."

    The movie was imitated by other studios, who did not do as well with the scenario. Because of its 1960s-era "anti-establishment" theme, *Easy Rider* became a cult classic.

*Wyatt (Peter Fonda) and George (Jack Nicholson) sit by campfire during cross-country journey in **Easy Rider**.*

Hannibal Hayes (Ben Murphy) and Kid Curry (Roger Davis) on set in Castle Valley during filming of "The Long Chase," a two-hour movie for the television series "Alias Smith and Jones."

"ALIAS SMITH AND JONES" - TV SERIES (1972)
  "THE LONG CHASE" (2-Hour Movie) and
  "HIGH AND LONESOME COUNTRY" (1-Hour Show)

NOTE: Scenes for six other segments of the "Alias Smith and Jones" series were also shot in Moab.

LOCATIONS: Castle Valley, Professor Valley, Potash Plant, and La Sal Mountains (Based in Moab)

CAST: Roger Davis, Ben Murphy, James Drury, Marie Windsor, Frank Sinatra, Jr., J.D. Cannon, Dean Jagger, Buddy Ebsen, and Rod Cameron.

ABOUT THE SERIES: Hannibal Hayes and Kid Curry are two bandits dodging the law while trying to get amnesty for prior crimes, which has been promised them by the Territorial Governor if they go one year without getting into trouble. The pair continuously stumble into situations where they are either suspected of a crime they didn't commit, or wind up getting involved in situations they can't resist. The light-hearted bad guys try to be good, but are always just one step ahead of the law as each segment comes to an end.

THE EIGER SANCTION (1974)

LOCATIONS: Monument Valley (Based at Goulding's Lodge, Utah) **NOTE:** Segments were also filmed in the Wasatch Mountains near Salt Lake City, Utah.

CAST: Clint Eastwood, George Kennedy, Vonetta McGee, Jack Cassidy, and Thayer David.

In a dangerous scene from **The Eiger Sanction**, *Clint Eastwood and George Kennedy, right, work with professional mountain climbers Mike Hoover and Peter Palafian, left.*

ABOUT THE MOVIE: The Technicolor film has a James Bond-type theme and characters. An art teacher, who was a former CIA agent, finds himself with a group mountain climbing on the Eiger in Switzerland. His former employers have asked him to return to the position of exterminator, and given him the "sanction" to kill for the good of his country. This exciting spy melodrama climaxes with some breathtaking mountain-climbing sequences.

AGAINST A CROOKED SKY (1975)

LOCATIONS: Professor Valley, Colorado River, Castle Valley, Arches National Park, Dead Horse Point (Based in Moab)

CAST: Richard Boone, Stewart Petersen, Henry Wilcoxon, Clint Ritchie, Shannon Farnon, Jewell Blanch, Brenda Benus, Geofrey Land, Gordon Hansen, Vincent St. Cyr, Margaret Willey, Norman Walki, Juanita Blackwater* and George Dale. *Local actress

ABOUT THE MOVIE: "In the dark shadows of history lie legends of lost civilizations whose kings ruled with power of the gods, only to crumble into the dust of time. From such a place rode three horsemen, their leader wearing the gold of ancient royalty." This dramatic narration at the opening of this technicolor Western helps establish the movie's theme.

A long-forgotten tribe of Indians invades the Sutter homestead when Sam, a scrappy boy of 11, and his 16-year-old sister, Charlotte, are alone. As the children attempt to get away, Charlotte is hurt and sends Sam for help. By the time he returns, the Indians have carried her away. The children's father searches unsuccessfully for his daughter and returns home convinced she is dead. Believing she's still alive, Sam runs away to continue the search. Displaying a gold headband dropped by the Indian who kidnaped Charlotte, Sam manages to entice Russian Habbakuk, a scruffy old drunken trapper, into joining him.

The pair get their first clue to Charlotte's whereabouts from an old Indian, his tongue cut out, who is living in shame with the Cheyenne. Using sign language, Cut Tongue offers to lead Sam and Russian to the tribe. Sam is greatly distressed when he finds that Charlotte, now married to the chief's son, Temkai, is unjustly accused of a crime against the tribe and is condemned to die. Sam offers his life in her place, then must pass the great test of courage that few warriors have been able to do. Sam completes his test but, returning a few seconds too late, he sees the arrow fly from the executioner's bow. With a hood over her head, he believes it is his sister who falls over a cliff edge to her death.

Months later, back at the Sutter homestead, Sam and his father are working in the fields when they see someone in the nearby willows. To their disbelief but great joy, it is Charlotte. Temkai has returned her to her family, along with their new child. It was a woman friend of Charlottes,' impressed with Sam's willingness to die in his sister's place, who had given her life for a friend.

Russian (Richard Boone) plays drunken trapper who helps rescue Charlotte.

Cut Tongue (Henry Wilcoxon), as Indian who leads Russian and Sam to Indian camp where Charlotte is held captive.

140

*Sam Sutter (Stewart Peterson) tries to help his injured sister Charlotte (Jewell Blanch) escape from Indians after she has fallen from horse, in dramatic opening scene of **Against A Crooked Sky**. Courtesy of The Times-Independent.*

Russian (Richard Boone) and Sam (Stewart Peterson) are trapped by a group of Indians as they search for young Charlotte. Courtesy of The Times-Independent.

SPACEHUNTER: ADVENTURES IN THE FORBIDDEN ZONE (1982)

LOCATIONS: Kane Creek, Bull Canyon, Colorado River, Lower Shafer Trail, Potash Settling Ponds, and Grey Hills, off U.S. Highway 191, south of Canyonlands Airport (Based in Moab)

CAST: Peter Strauss, Molly Ringwald, Ernie Hudson, John Wildman, Paul Boretski, Beeson Carroll, Deborah Pratt, Cali Timmins, Aliesa Shirley, Vince Deadrick, Jr., Rock Walker, Andrea Marcovicci, Michael Ironside, Hrant Alianak, and Reggie Bennett.

Actor Peter Strauss (Wolff) in scene from **Spacehunter**. *Courtesy of The Times-Independent.*

ABOUT THE MOVIE: *Spacehunter* is the story of a wily mercenary named Wolff, who responds to a galactic distress signal that promises a fortune to the pilot who rescues three maidens marooned on the plague-ravaged planet of Terra 11.

The 3-D movie opens with a spin through space, as a shuttle makes an emergency crash-landing on Terra 11. When a lovely trio of space girls departs from their craft, a mob of "Trikers" surrounds and abducts them.

Back aboard Wolff's spaceship, the radio communicator blows just as a mayday message from the girls' craft starts to come in. Since Wolff is a galaxy-hopping garbage collector, he assumes the signal is just another call for a beryllium waste pickup. He calls on Chalmers, his charming robot companion, to fix the radio.

As the distress call comes through, Wolff learns that the first exploration party went to Terra 11 in the year 2013. They were hit by a plague in 2021 and an inter-planetary plague control group was sent in 2022 to assist them. This was led by two men, Patterson and McNabb (alias Overdog). McNabb assumed dictatorship of the planet. It is also learned that a medical expedition sent in 2031 had vanished. Since that time, the planet had been quarantine-restricted. With the stakes high for the girls' return, Wolff and Chalmers blast off for the forbidden target. After a successful landing, they hop in their land-roving machine to search for the ladies in peril.

Creatures from the sky have carried the space maidens off to the forbidden zone, and Wolff finds himself in a battle for his life. Chalmers is destroyed, and Wolff meets up with Niki, a young spitfire orphan who claims she knows the planet and will be willing to guide him to the forbidden zone in exchange for something to eat.

The two encounter all kinds of creatures in the monster-infested underground during their search. They dislike each other, but also share a mutual respect. Niki is always trying to "brain work" Wolff and he is bothered by her attitude. Wolff makes clear their relationship is only an exchange of food for taking him to the forbidden zone. In the closing scenes, the space girls are rescued and Wolff, who now understands Niki's behavior is due to loneliness, asks her to come with him away from Terra 11.

142

Cali Timmons, Aliesa Shirley and Deborah Pratt play a trio of lovely space maidens shipwrecked on a plague-ravaged planet in Columbia Pictures' 3-D action-thriller **Spacehunter: Adventures in the Forbidden Zone**.

One of the plague victims on Terra Eleven, in battle scene from movie **Spacehunter**. *Courtesy of Tony Osusky (standing center).*

CHOKE CANYON (1984)

LOCATIONS: Moab City: Fourth East; Byrd's Ranch near the portal of the Colorado River, Onion Creek, Professor Valley, Sand Flats, Dead Horse Point, Squaw Park (Based in Moab)

CAST: Stephen Collins, Janet Julian, Bo Svenson, Lance Henricksen, Victoria Racimo, and Nicholas Pryor.

Biplane lands on Fourth East in Moab, Utah, during chase sequence in **Choke Canyon**. *Photo by Bego Gerhart.*

ABOUT THE MOVIE: A physicist, David Lowell, is hoping to solve the world's energy problems. He believes that when Halley's Comet passes over Choke Canyon in 1986 it will create maximum distortion of sound waves in the canyon, and he will be able to harness energy from the effect.

Lowell has a 99-year lease on the site where his lab is located, but Pilgrim Corporation, which owns the land, wants to use the canyon as a secret dump for nuclear waste from some of its operations. When Lowell refuses to budge, Mr. Pilgrim sends in his hitman, known as "Captain."

Lowell manages to outwit Captain and finally kidnaps Pilgrim's daughter in a desperate attempt to hold the corporation at bay while he completes his experiment. The young woman is won over to the cause, and before the comet arrives, there is a series of spectacular aerial chase sequences between a biplane and a helicopter, dangling Pilgrim's nuclear waste on a cable below. In the final scenes, Lowell completes his experiment and then delivers the nuclear waste to the Utah state capitol, dropping it in the lap of the governor.

Crew gears for a close-up shot of Lowell battling for his life on large black ball containing nuclear waste. In the movie **Choke Canyon**, *they appear to be high above the canyons off Dead Horse Point, dangling beneath a helicopter. Photo by Bego Gerhart.*

Scene at historic Dewey Bridge, where the biplane flies under and the helicopter with ball and stuntman go over the bridge, during aerial dog fight. Photo by Bego Gerhart.

NIGHTMARE AT NOON (1987)

LOCATIONS: Moab City: Courthouse and jail, Canyonlands Cafe, Grand-Vu Drive-In Theater, and Center Street; Ken's Lake, Colorado River, and Arches National Park (Based in Moab)

CAST: George Kennedy, Bo Hopkins, Wings Hauser, Kimberly Beck, Kimberly Ross, Brion James, *Nik Hougen, *Larry Campbell, *Sheri Griffith, *Pete Plastow, *Karl Tangren, *Alan West and *Doug Morck. * Local Actors

Deputy Sheriff Julia Hanks (Kimberly Ross) comforts wounded Ken Griffins (Wings Hauser) following a gun battle in scene from **Nightmare At Noon**.

ABOUT THE MOVIE: The story mixes toxic warfare with good old-fashioned Western elements. Unknown agents, presumed to be from some foreign country, poison the drinking water in the small western town of Canyonlands. One by one the residents go berserk and when wounded, bleed green fluid. As Sheriff Hanks and his deputy daughter Julia attempt to keep order in their city, the situation grows worse.

Cheri and Ken Griffins, who get stranded in Canyonlands while on vacation, are joined by a hitchhiker, Riley, picked up en route to town. The trio unites forces with Sheriff Hanks and Julia in an effort to find out who or what is responsible for the bizarre happenings. As it turns out, Riley is an ex-police officer who has quit the force after killing someone in the line of duty (a fellow cop who was trying to rape a young girl).

Cheri Griffins, who earlier drank water in a cafe, tries to kill anyone who comes near her. She must be locked up in jail for her own safety, as well as that of others. Sheriff Hanks, who had water in his morning coffee, dies a violent death, not only from the poison but because he is torched by the villains, who have finally come out of hiding. Lead by a character called the Albino, the foreign troops then desert their high-tech vans and escape on horseback into the desert. Deputy Julia Hanks, Riley, and Ken find some horses and head out after them.

146

Ken is wounded and Riley goes on alone, while Julia stays with Ken. Just as Riley and the Albino come face-to-face for a shoot-out, a menacing black helicopter appears in the sky behind the Albino. Just as suddenly a military helicopter, responding to an earlier distress call, also appears on the horizon, and a dogfight between the two crafts takes on dazzling proportions over some of the world's most beautiful landscapes (Arches National Park).

Meanwhile, Riley has wounded the Albino and forces him to take a poison capsule like the ones used to contaminate the town's water. Case solved, the battle won, Cheri Griffins recovers and the couple prepare to move on. Riley, momentarily torn between Julia and the open road, gives her a kiss and bids her adieu, as he joins the Griffins.

The Albino (Brion James) during final showdown scene with Riley in **Nightmare At Noon**.

SUNDOWN: VAMPIRES IN RETREAT (1988)

LOCATIONS: Moab, Thompson Springs, Spanish Valley, Hittle Bottom, Arches National Park (Based in Moab)

CAST: David Carradine, John Ireland, Morgan Brittany, Maxwell Caulfield, Deborah Foreman, Jim Metzler, *Vanessa Pierson, Erin Gourlay, Lloyd "Sunshine" Parker, M. Emmet Walsh, Buck Flower, Bruce Campbell, Paul Harper, Geraldo Mejia, Marion Eaton, Dana Ashbrook, Elizabeth Gracen, Helena Carroll, Mike Jajjar, Jack (Jones) Eiseman, Christopher Bradley. * Local Actress

ABOUT THE MOVIE: The movie is best described as a contemporary/vampire/western comedy satire. The story is about a small Arizona community named Purgatory, which has, as is soon revealed, a population of good vampires and bad vampires. The good guys manufacture their blood at the local "technoplasma" plant. The bad guys prefer the real thing, and are trying to take over the town and go back to their old ways.

Caught up in all of this, and at first unaware that they are in the midst of vampires, is the Harrison family. Mr. Harrison, who had developed the artificial blood, has come to town to check on the progress of the plasma factory, accompanied by his wife and two daughters. **NOTE:** This movie appeared on video, only.

Principal extras as residents of Purgatory in **Sundown: Vampires in Retreat.**

Purgatory police officer, standing watch in the desert during filming of **Sundown.** *Courtesy of Sheri Griffith.*

INDIANA JONES AND THE LAST CRUSADE (1988)

LOCATIONS: Arches National Park (Park Avenue and Windows Section), Sevenmile Canyon (Based in Moab and Green River, Utah)

CAST: Harrison Ford, River Phoenix (playing Indiana Jones as a boy); Stars not on location in Moab but in the feature include: Sean Connery, Denholm Elliott, Alison Doody, John Rhys-Davis, and Julian Glover.

ABOUT THE MOVIE: This George Lucas/Steven Spielberg spectacular broke all box office records, taking in $50-million during the first week of release. Director Steven Spielberg claimed this was the last of the Indiana Jones movies.

In this round of adventure, Indiana is joined by his father and reflects back on his childhood. It is 1912 and Jones (River Phoenix) is on a Boy Scout trip. While exploring a cave, he and his friends discover a group of grave robbers who have just found Coronado's Cross. Feeling strongly that the cross belongs in a museum, Jones steals the valuable artifact and the chase begins. (The flashback is the sequence filmed in Moab and is used as the dynamic opening for the picture.)

The movie is packed with suspense and adventure. In later action, Jones discovers the existence of the Holy Grail and the disappearance of his father, who has been searching for the mythical grail. By reading his father's diary, Jones is able to trace him.

*Director Steven Spielberg and River Phoenix (playing Indiana Jones when he was young) prepare for a shot at the entrance of Sevenmile Canyon, during filming of **Indiana Jones and the Last Crusade.***

Young Indiana Jones (River Phoenix) in **Indiana Jones and the Last Crusade** *scene filmed at Double Arch in Arches National Park.*

NOTE: River Phoenix returned in 1993 to film ***Dark Blood***, with key locations in the Factory Butte area around Hanksville, Utah. The company completed filming at this location and was in the process of moving to the next location when Phoenix met his untimely death. He was on break in California at the time. It is uncertain whether the movie will ever be completed.

THELMA AND LOUISE (1990)

LOCATIONS: La Sal, Cisco, Thompson Springs, old Valley City reservoir (dry lake bed), Potash Trail and Arches National Park; also just over the border in Colorado near Grand Junction and Bedrock. (Based in Moab) **NOTE:** The promotional piece used for movie was shot in Monument Valley.

CAST: Geena Davis, Susan Sarandon, Harvey Keitel, Michael Madsen, Christopher McDonald and Brad Pitt.

ABOUT THE MOVIE: This is a female "road" movie about two gals who decide to get away for a long weekend and wind up on a crime spree that ends in disaster. Thelma is a housewife whose husband exemplifies the traditional not-too-bright male, who has a way of making his wife feel she is less than brilliant and can't get along without him. Her pal, Louise, initially the stronger personality of the two, is a waitress with a live-in boyfriend, who is unable to make a permanent commitment. Both women feel the need to get away and make plans to do so.

En route to their vacation spot, Thelma and Louise stop off at a roadhouse for a drink. Thelma's naive flirtations are mistaken for a come-on by a local dude who figures himself a real stud. He follows Thelma outside to the parking lot, where he attempts to rape her. Louise appears on the scene, draws a gun, and shoots the offender. There is a subtle hint that something dreadful had happened to Louise earlier in her life, which triggered the spontaneous reaction to the offender.

*In **Thelma and Louise**, female fugitives go airborne in dramatic attempt to elude posse. A rim below Dead Horse Point, on the Potash Trail, doubled for the Grand Canyon in this scene. Photo by Diane Nagel.*

At this point, the fun-loving mood of the film changes. Feeling that no one will believe what happened in the parking lot, the girls decide to make a run for the Mexican border. Louise suffers great remorse over the incident. Fearing the consequences and after several set-backs in their escape plan, she eventually loses her take-charge capability. In the meantime, Thelma seems to be having the time of her life. Meeting a cute hitchhiker, Thelma agrees to give him a ride. Thelma has an intimate encounter with the guy (a convenience-store bandit), who then runs off with Louise's life savings - money that was meant to get the women to Mexico.

During the relationship with the hitchhiker, Thelma learns how to rob convenience stores, and proceeds to do so after Louise's money is stolen. Her excitement grows with each caper, and Louise becomes more despondent.

By this time, the FBI is on the case, Thelma's husband is frantic, and Louise's boyfriend is learning what it's like to wait while his lover is on-the-road. A kindly cop, understanding the circumstances surrounding the killing, is trying to catch the girls before their odyssey turns tragic.

While the women continue their self-destructive escapades, the posse is in relentless pursuit, finally trapping the fugitives on a cliff edge. The women consider their options - a prison stretch versus the plunge ahead of them. It's life or death. In their last act of free choice, Thelma and Louise clasp hands and the accelerator hits the floor.

Louise (Susan Sarandon) shares scene with old-time Cisco resident, Ernest Vanderhoff. Although he had no lines, the scene was touching. Traveling a scorching hot desert, Louise trades her jewelry for the man's hat.

GERONIMO: AN AMERICAN LEGEND (1993)

LOCATIONS: Professor Valley, Potash Trail, Needles Overlook area, Onion Creek, the sand dunes off Ruby Ranch road, Bates Ranch, and the Lawson Ranch. (Based in Moab)

CAST: Jason Patric, Gene Hackman, Robert Duvall, Wes Studi, Matt Damon, Rodney A. Grant, Kevin Tighe, Steve Reevis, Carlos Palomino, Victor Aaron, Stuart "Proud Eagle" Grant, Stephen McHattie, John Finn, Lee De Brouix, Reno Thunder, Hoke Howell, Richard Martin, Jr., J. Young, Raleigh Wilson, Jackie Old Coyote, Monty Bass, Pato Hoffman, Scott Crabbe, Patricia Pretzinger, Roger Callard, Judson Keith Linn, Mark Boone Junior, M.C. Gainey, Michael Rudd, Michael Minjarez, Burnette Bennett, *Davina Smith, Jonathan Ward, Luis Contreras, Jacquelin Lee, Jim Many Goats, Scott Wilson, Eva Larson, Greg Goossen, Sonny Skyhawk, Michael Adams, Walter Robles, Anthony Schmidt, Jim Beaver. *(local actress)

ABOUT THE MOVIE: The movie focuses on the final months of the U.S. Army's Geronimo campaign of 1885-86, with its efforts to subjugate the last of the free Apache. Only four bands of Chiricahua Apache remained, living a nomadic existence throughout the territories of Arizona, New Mexico, and Mexico. Their great leaders - Cochise, Victorio, Delgadito and Mangas Colorado - were all dead by this time.

Under the leadership Geronimo, the Chiricahua Apache continue to fight for their land and freedom. A respected war leader and medicine man, Geronimo is the key figure in a series of events that play out a full social and cultural tragedy.

Lieutenant Charles Gatewood is charged with negotiating Geronimo's final surrender. During his pursuit, the viewer becomes aware of the ambivalent bond that forms between the Apache and the cavalry charged with breaking their spirit. Geronimo bravely leads his people against a formidable force of U.S. Army troops and Mexican soldiers, until he is brought to his final surrender.

Director/producer Walter Hill made every effort to assure historical authenticity, which included having a Native American consultant team on set. While Hill takes nominal historic liberties of both a sequential and interpretive nature, he notes that the story deals with the "legend." Noted historian on the American West, John Langellier, says of the film: "There are a few historical inaccuracies...but those are overwhelmed by the authenticity..., which exceeds anything ever seen in a Western. The movie, then, is a milestone in filmmaking."

Preparing for scene at San Carlos where Dead Shot (Monty Bass) and two other Apaches from Cibecue Creek are to be hung by the cavalry. Photo by Cindi Stevenson.

Geronimo (Wes Studi) meets with General Crook and his men. Photo by Darlene Smith.

*Cavalry mounts up for drill at San Carlos in scene from **Geronimo: An American Legend**. Photo by Cindi Stevenson.*

A band of Chiricahua Apache charge a lone wagon in the Geronimo feature.

Cavalry at Fort San Carlos is loading Geronimo and other Apaches in wagons to meet the train and transport them to Florida. Photo by Cindi Stevenson.

Indians await encounter with **Lightning Jack** *(Paul Hogan) in movie of the same name. Photo by Lynn Stones.*

Scene from **City Slickers II: The Search for Curly's Gold**, *a Castle Rock Production. Photo by Bego Gerhart.*

*Rachel McLish, flung from wrecked van, is on fire in scene from **Raven Hawk**, filmed by Weatherly Productions. Photo by B.J. Griffith.*

*Stars Ted Danson and young Ryan Todd in Pontiac convertible, on location in Professor Valley during filming of **Pontiac Moon**. Photo by Lynn Stones.*

Movie & Television Highlights
Over 120 Movies and TV Series Filmed in the Moab-Monument Valley Area
All dates given for Moab area are when filmed, Monument Valley movies have release dates.
* Movies with one-third or less filmed in the area. ** Locals who were cast as "day players" or in principal roles.

1925 – *The Vanishing American** - Paramount Pictures
Director: George B. Seitz
Starring: Richard Dix, Lois Wilson, Noah Beery
Location: Monument Valley

1939 – *Stagecoach* – United Artists
Director: John Ford
Starring: John Wayne, Claire Trevor, Thomas Mitchell, John Carradine, Louise Platt, George Bancroft, Tim Holt, Tom Tyler, Francis Ford, Yakima Canutt, Chief Big Tree, Andy Devine, John Carradine
Location: Monument Valley.

1940 – *Kit Carson* – United Artists
Director: George B. Seitz
Starring: Jon Hall, Dana Andrews, Ward Bond, Clayton Moore, Lynn Bari, Renee Raino
Location: Monument Valley

1941 - *Billy The Kid** – Metro Goldwyn Mayer Studio
Director: David Miller
Starring: Robert Taylor, Brian Donlevy, Henry O'Neill, Mary Howard, Gene Lockhart
Locations: Monument Valley (also Sedona, Arizona)

1946 – *The Harvey Girls** - MGM Studio
Director: George Sidney
Starring: Judy Garland, John Hodiak, Angela Lansbury, Preston Foster, Ray Bolger,
Location: Monument Valley

1925 – *The Vanishing American** - Paramount Pictures
Director: George B. Seitz
Starring: Richard Dix, Lois Wilson, Noah Beery
Location: Monument Valley

1939 – *Stagecoach* – United Artists
Director: John Ford
Starring: John Wayne, Claire Trevor, Thomas Mitchell, John Carradine, Louise Platt, George Bancroft, Tim Holt, Tom Tyler, Francis Ford, Yakima Canutt, Chief Big Tree, Andy Devine, John Carradine
Location: Monument Valley.

1940 – *Kit Carson* – United Artists
Director: George B. Seitz
Starring: Jon Hall, Dana Andrews, Ward Bond, Clayton Moore, Lynn Bari, Renee Raino
Location: Monument Valley

1941 - *Billy The Kid** – Metro Goldwyn Mayer Studio
Director: David Miller
Starring: Robert Taylor, Brian Donlevy, Henry

1946 – *My Darling Clementine* – 20th Century Fox
Director: John Ford
Starring: Henry Fonda, Victor Mature, Walter Brennan, Linda Darnell, Cathy Downs, Ward Bond, Tim Holt, John Ireland, Jane Darwell, Russell Simpson, Francis Ford
Location: Monument Valley

1948 – *Fort Apache* – RKO Radio
Director: John Ford
Starring: John Wayne, Henry Fonda, Shirley Temple, John Agar, Pedro Armendariz, George O'Brien, Anna Lee, Ward Bond, Victor McLaglen, Ben Johnson, Francis Ford
Locations: Monument Valley, San Juan River

1949 – *She Wore a Yellow Ribbon* – RKO/Argosy
Director: John Ford
Starring: John Wayne, Joanne Dru, John Agar, Ben Johnson, George O'Brien, Victor McLaglen, Harry Carey, Jr., Mildred Natwick, Francis Ford, Tom Tyler, Chief Big Tree
Locations: Monument Valley, San Juan River at Mexican Hat

1949 – *Wagonmaster* – Argosy Pictures/RKO
Director: John Ford
Starring: Ben Johnson, Harry Carey, Jr., Joanne Dru, Ward Bond, Jane Darwell, Russell Simpson, Kathleen O'Malley, James Arness, Francis Ford, Ruth Clifford, Charles Kemper
Locations: Professor Valley, Colorado River, Spanish Valley, Fisher Towers, Locomotive Rock

1950 – *Rio Grande* – Republic/Argosy Pictures
Director: John Ford
Starring: John Wayne, Maureen O'Hara, Claude Jarman, Jr., Harry Carey, Jr., Ben Johnson, Victor McLaglen, J. Carrol Naish, Chill Wills, Patrick Wayne
Locations: White Ranch (Red Cliff), Onion Ckeek, Ida Gulch, Professor Valley, Colorado River

1952 – *Battle At Apache Pass* – Universal-International
Director: George Sherman
Starring: Jeff Chandler, John Lund, Susan Cabot,

Hugh O'Brian, Richard Egan, Jack Elam, Jay Silverheels, Bruce Cowling
Locations: Courthouse Wash, Ida Gulch, Professor Valley, Colorado River, Sand Flats, Arches National Monument (NM)

1953 – *Border River* – Universal-International
Director: George Sherman
Starring: Joel McCrea, Yvonne De Carlo, Alfonso Bedoya, Pedro Armendariz, Ivan Triesault, Howard Petrie, Lane Chandler
Locations: Professor Valley, Colorado River, White Ranch (Red Cliff), Courthouse Wash

1953 – *Taza, Son of Cochise* – Universal-International
Director: Douglas Sirk
Starring: Rock Hudson, Barbara Rush, Jeff Chandler, Gene Iglesias, **Barbara Burck
Locations: White Ranch (Red Cliff), Castle Valley, Professor Valley, Sand Flats

1953 – *Siege At Red River* – 20th Century Fox
Director: Rudollph Mate
Starring: Van Johnson, Joanne Dru, Richard Boone, Jeff Marrow, Milburn Stone, Craig Hill
Locations: Professor Valley, Locomotive Rock, Colorado River, Castle Valley (also Durango, Colorado)

1954 – *Smoke Signal* – Universal-International
Director: Jerry Hooper
Starring: Dana Andrews, Piper Laurie, William Talman, Rex Reason, Milburn Stone
Locations: Big Bend/Colorado River, Professor Valley, Hauer Ranch, Ida Gulch, San Juan River

1954 – *Canyon Crossroads* – United Artists/MPTC Prod.
Director: Alfred L. Werker
Starring: Richard Basehart, Phyllis Kirk, Stephen Elliott, Russell Collins, Charles Wagenheim
Locations: Moab City, Professor Valley, Sevenmile Canyon (a Moab uranium boom story)

1956 – *Fort Dobbs* - Warner Brothers
Director: Gordon Douglas
Starring: Clint Walker, Virginia Mayo, Brian Keith, Michael Dante, Brian Keith, Richard Eyer
Locations: Colorado River, Matt Martin Wash, Professor Valley (also at Kanab, Utah)

1956 – *The Searchers* – Warner Brothers
Director: John Ford
Starring: John Wayne, Jeffrey Hunter, Harry Carey, Jr., Vera Miles, Ward Bond, Natalie Wood, John Qualen, Olive Carey, Patrick Wayne, Hank Worden, Henry Brandon
Locations: Monument Valley, San Juan River at Mexican Hat

1958 – *Warlock* - 20th Century Fox
Director: Edward Dmytryk
Starring: Henry Fonda, Anthony Quinn, Richard

Widmark, Dorothy Malone
Locations: Professor Valley, Dead Horse Point State Park (SP), Kings Bottom, Doles/Bates Ranch, Arches NM, Sand Flats

1959 – *Ten Who Dared* – Walt Disney Studios
Director: William Beaudine
Starring: John Beal, Brian Keith, Ben Johnson, L.Q. Jones, **George E. White
Locations: Big Bend of the Colorado River, White Ranch (Red Cliff), Arches NM, Dead Horse Point SP

1960 – *Gold of the Seven Saints* – Warner Brothers
Director: Gordon Douglas
Starring: Clint Walker, Roger Moore, Chill Wills, Gene Evens, Leticia Morman
Locations:: Fisher Towers, Colorado River, White Ranch (Red Cliff), Sevenmile Wash, Klondike Flats, Arches NM

1960 – *Sergeant Rutledge* – Warner Brothers
Director: John Ford
Starring: Jeffrey Hunter, Constance Towers, Woody Strode, Mae Marsh, Eva Novak
Locations: Monument Valley, San Juan River

1961 – *The Comancheros* – 20th Century Fox
Director: Michael Curtiz
Starring: John Wayne, Stuart Whitman, Ina Balin, Nehemiah Persoff, Lee Marvin, Shirley Jones, Patrick Wayne, Michael Ansara, Bruce Cabot, Jack Elam
Locations: Professor Valley, Dead Horse SP, Kings Bottom, La Sal Mountains, Fisher Valley, Onion Creek, Fisher Towers

1963 – *The Greatest Story Ever Told* - Geo. Stevens Prod.
Director: George Stevens
Starring: Max von Sydow, Charlton Heston, Carroll Baker, Angela Lansbury, Sidney Poitier, Shelley Winters, John Wayne, Van Heflin, Claude Rains, Telly Savalas
Locations: Island in the Sky, Green River Overlook, (also areas around Page, Arizona)

1963 – *Cheyenne Autumn* – Warner Brothers
Director: John Ford
Starring: Richard Widmark, Carroll Baker, Ricardo Montalban, Gilbert Roland, Sal Mineo, Victor Jory, Dolores Del Rio, Karl Malden, Patrick Wayne, Ben Johnson, Harry Carey, Jr., James Stewart, Arthur Kennedy, John Carradine, Elizabeth Allen
Locations: White Ranch (Red Cliff), Castle Valley, Professor Valley, Colorado River, Fisher Canyon, Arches NM, Mexican Hat, San Juan River, Monument Valley

1964 – *Rio Conchos* – 20th Century Fox
Director: Gordon Douglas
Starring: Richard Boone, Stuart Whitman, Edmund

Locations: O'Brien, Anthony Franciosa, Jim Brown
White Ranch (Red Cliff), Professor Valley, Castle Valley, Arches NP, Dead Horse Point SP

1966 – *Wild Rovers* * - MGM Studio
Director: Blake Edwards
Starring: William Holden, Ryan O'Neal. Karl Malden
Locations: Arches NM, Monument Valley

1967 – *Blue* – Paramount Pictures
Director: Silvio Narizzano
Starring: Terence Stamp, Ricardo Montalban, Karl Malden, Joanna Pettet, ** Iva Lou Redd
Location: Professor Valley, Colorado River, La Sal Mountains, Sevenmile Canyon, Redd Ranch, Wood Ranch, Sand Flats

1967 – *Fade In* – B.C.W. Productions
Director: Jud Taylor
Starring: Burt Reynolds, Barbara Loden, Noam Pitnik, Patricia Casey, James Hampton
Locations: Moab City, Professor Valley, Dole/Bates Ranch (story of *Blue* filmed at Moab.)

1968 – *2001: A Space Odyssey* * - Larry Spangler Prod.
Director: Stanley Kubrik
Starring: Keir Dullea, Gary Lockwood
Location: Monument Valley

1969 – *Easy Rider* * - Larry Spangler Productions
Director: Dennis Hopper
Starring: Peter Fonda, Dennis Hopper, Jack Nicholson
Location: Monument Valley

1969 – *Mackenna's Gold* * - Columbia Pictures
Director: J. Lee Thompson
Starring: Gregory Peck, Omar Sharif, Telly Savalas, Camilla Sparv, Eli Wallach, Kennan Wynn, Raymond Massey, Lee J. Cobb
Location: Monument Valley

1970 – *Run Cougar Run* – Disney Studios
Director: Jerry Courtland
Starring: Stuart Whitman, Harry Carey, Jr.
Locations: Castle Valley, La Sal Mountains, Arches NM

1971 – *Vanishing Point* – 20th Century Fox/Cupid Prod.
Director: Richard C. Sarafian
Starring: Barry Newman, Dean Jagger, Victoria Medlin, Cleavon Little
Locations: Thompson Springs, Cisco, along Highway Interstate-70

1973 – *Electra Glide in Blue* * - Tomorrow Entertainment
Director: James William Guercio
Starring: Robert Blake, Billy Green Bush, Mitchell Ryan
Location: Monument Valley

1972 – *Alias Smith and Jones* – Universal Studios (TV Pilot, plus several episodes)

Director: Alexander Singer
Starring: Roger Davis, Ben Murphy, J. D. Cannon, Buddy Ebsen, Marie Windsor, Frank Sinatra. Jr., Dean Jagger, Rod Cameron
Locations: Castle Valley, Professor Valley, La Sal Mountains, Potash Plant area

1975 – *Against A Crooked Sky* – Doty Dayton Productions
Director: Earl Bellamy
Starring: Richard Boone, Stewart Peterson, Henry Wilcoxon, Shannon Farnon, Jewell Blanch, Clint Richi, ** Juanita Blackwater, **Eric Bjornstad
Locations: Professor Valley, Castle Valley, Colorado River, Arches NP, Dead Horse Point SP

1979 – *The Villain* * - Columbia Pictures
Director: Hal Needham
Starring: Kirk Douglas, Ann-Margaret, Jack Elam,
Location: Monument Valley

1980 – *My Road* – Dakota Lines Productions
Director: Kikuo Kawasake
Starring: Tatsuya Nakadai, Yaysuki Takito
Locations: Moab City, Dead Horse Point SP

1981 – *The Legend of the Lone Ranger* * - Universal Studios
Director: William A. Fraker
Starring: Klinton Spilsbury, Jason Robards, Richard Farnsworth
Locations: Monument Valley, Marble Arch

1982 – *Spacehunter: Adventures in the Forbidden Zone* – Zone Productions/Colummbia Pictures
Director: Lamont Johnson
Starring: Peter Strauss, Molly Ringwald, Ernie Hudson, Andrea Marcovicci, Michael Ironside, Beeson Carroll, Deborah Platt
Locations: Kane Creek, Bull Canyon, Colorado River, Potash area, lower Shafer Trail, Grey Hills

1983 – *National Lampoon's Vacation* * - Paramount Pictures
Director: Harold Ramis
Starring: Chevy Chase, Beverly D'Angelo, Anthony Michael Hall, Imogene Coca
Location: Monument Valley

1984 – *Choke Canyon* – Brouwersgrat Inv.
Director: Chuck Ball
Starring: Stephen Collins, Janet Julien, Bo Svenson,
Locations: Moab City, Onion Creek, Professor Valley, Sand Flats, Dead Horse Point SP, Byrd Ranch, Squaw Park

1985 – *MacGyver* * – Paramount Pictures (TV Pilot)
Director: Jerrold Freedman
Starring: Richard Dean Anderson
Locations: Dead Horse Point SP, Shafer Overlook

1986 – *Jack Tillman: The Survivalist* – Lodestar Productions
Director: Sig Shore
Starring: Cliff De Young, Susan Blakely, Steve

Railsback, Marjo Gortner, David Wayne, **Ron Trimble, ** Terra Trimble, ** Fred Hampton

Locations: Pack Creek Ranch, Onion Creek, Moab City, La Sal Mountains, Spanish Valley

1987 – *Nightmare At Noon* – Omega/Inhaus
Director: Nico Mastorakis
Starring: George Kennedy, Bo Hopkins, Wings Hauser, Kimberly Beck, Kimberly Ross, Brion James,** Nik Hougen, **Larry Campbell, ** Sheri Griffith, **Alan West, **Pete Plastow, **Karl Tangren, **Doug Morck
Locations: Moab City, Ken's Lake, Arches NP, Colorado River

1988 – *Sundown: Vampires in Retreat* – Vestron/Sundown
Director: Anthony Hickox
Starring: John Ireland, David Carradine, Morgan Brittany, Maxwell Caulfield, Deborah Foreman, Jim Metzler, **Vanessa Pierson
Locations: Thompson Springs, Moab City, Spanish Valley, Hittle Bottom, Arches NP

1988 – *Indiana Jones and the Last Crusade* - LUCASFilms
Director: Steven Spielberg
Starring: Harrison Ford, Sean Connery, River Phoenix, Dunholm Elliott, Alison Doody, John Ras-Davis, Julian Glover
Locations: Arches NP, Sevenmile Canyon

1990 – *Thelma and Louise* – Percy Main Productions
Director: Ridley Scott
Starring: Geena Davis, Susan Sarandon, Harvey Kietel, Michael Madsen, Christopher McDonald, Brad Pitt, **Ernest Vonderhoff
Locations: Shafer Overlook, Arches NP, La Sal, Cisco, Thompson Springs, Valley City, Fossil Point

1990 – *Back To the Future III* - Paradox Productions
Director: Robert Zemeckis
Starring: Michael J. Fox, Christopher Lloyd
Location: Monument valley

1991 – *Equinos* - The Identical Company
Director: Alan Rudolph
Starring: Mathew Modine, Jennifer Grey
Locations: Crescent Junction, Moab City

1992 – *Knights* - Kings Road Entertainment
Director: Albert Pyun
Starring: Kris Kristofferson, Kathy Long, Lance Henrickson, Jon Epstein, Scott Paulen
Locations: Pucker Pass, Long Canyon, Professor Valley, Onion Creek, Needles Overlook, Church Rock, La Sal Mountains

1992 – *This Boy's Life* - Warner Brothers
Director: Michael Caton-James
Starring: Ellen Barkin, Leonardo DiCaprio, Robert DeNiro

Locations: La Sal Mountains Loop Road, Moab City

1992 – *Double Jeopardy* - Laurel Films (TV Movie)
Director: Lawrence Shiller
Starring: Bruce Boxleitner, Rachel Ward, Sela Ward
Locations: Highway 279, Rainbow Rocks

1992 – *Josh and S. A. M* - Castle Rock Pictures
Director: Billy Weber
Starring: Noah Fleiss, Jacob Tierney, Martha Pimpton
Locations: Arches NP, Highway 191, Lisbon Valley, Spanish Valley, Moab City

1992 – *Slaughter of the Innocents* - SGE Entertainment
Director: James Glickenhaus
Starring: Scott Glenn, Sheila Tousey, Jesse Cameron
Locations: Castle Rock, Onion Creek, Marie Ogden Settlement (also in Salt Lake City, Utah)

1993 – *Tall Tales* - Disney Productions
Director: Jeremiah Chechik
Starring: Patrick Swayze, Oliver Platt, Nick Stahi, Roger Aaron Brown, Catherine O'Hara, Moira Harris, William H. Macy, Jared Harris, Steven Lang
Locations: Monument Valley, San Juan River

1993 – *City Slickers II: The Search for Curly's Gold* – Columbia Pictures
Director: Paul Weiland
Starring: Billy Crystal, Jack Palance, Daniel Stern, Jon Lovitz, Patricia Wettig
Locations: Hauer Ranch, Fisher Towers, Onion Creek, Indian Creek, Dugout Ranch

1993 – *Geronimo: An American Legend* – Columbia
Director: Walter Hill
Starring: Wes Studi, Jason Patric, Robert Duvall, Gene Hackman, Rodney A. Grant, Stuart Grant, Matt Damon, **Davina Smith, **John Hagner
Location: Professor Valley, Potash Trail, Needles Overlook, White Wash Sand Dunes, Onion Creek, Dole/Bates Ranch, Lawson Ranch

1993 – *Forrest Gump* - Paramount Pictures/Raleigh Studios
Director: Robert Zemeckis
Starring: Tom Hanks, Robin Wright, Sally Fields, Gary Finise
Locations: Monument Valley, Valley of the Gods

1993 – *Pontiac Moon* - Paramount Pictures
Director: Peter Medak
Starring: Ted Danson, Mary Steenburgen, Ryan Todd
Locations: Arches NP, Cisco, Crescent Junction, Ruby Ranch Road, Monument Valley

1994 – *The Great American West* - Vineyard Productions
Director: Sterling Wagenen (an IMAX picture)
Starring: (undergoing research) **Tonia Brown
Locations: Monument Valley, Ida Gulch, Hauer Ranch, Fossil Point, Pucker Pass, Hook'n Ladder

1995 – *Larger Than Life* – MGM/United Artist
Director: Howard Franklin
Starring: Bill Murray and Tia, an elephant
Locations: Dole/Bates Ranch (Mexican village set), Shafer Trail, Professor Valley, off Highway 191 and 313, Green River City, Floy Wash, White Wash Sand Dunes

1995 – *Sunchasers** - Warner Brothers
Director: Michael Cimino
Starring: Woody Harrelson, Anne Bancroft, Jon Seda
Locations: Highway 128, Ida Gulch, Kane Creek, Shafer Trail, Long Canyon

1995 – *Riders of the Purple Sage* – TBS/VHS Productions
Director: Charlie Haid (TV movie)
Starring: Ed Harris, Amy Madigan, Henry Thomas, Robin Tunney, **Stephanie Griffith
Locations: Dugout Ranch (key set), Flat Pass, Mill Creek Canyon, Kane Springs Road, Ten Mile area, Pucker Pass

1995 – *Cheyenne* – Halo Productions (TV movie)
Director: Dimitri Logothetis
Starring: Gary Hudson, M. C. Hammer, Bo Svenson, Bobbie Phillips, Robert Bell, ** Verle Green
Locations: Hauer Ranch (key set/town and mine) Arches NP, Dead Horse Point SP, Highway 313, Thompson

1996 – *A Passion in the Desert* – Roland Films
Director: Lavinia Currer
Starring: Ben Daniels and Mogli, a leopard
Locations: Mill Creek Canyon, Flat Pass Long Canyon, White Wash Sand Dunes

1996 – *Breakdown* - Breakdown Productions
Director: Jonathan Mostow
Starring: Kurt Russel, Kathleen Quinlan
Locations: Professor Valley, Highway 313, Texaco. Station off Highway 191

1996 – *Con-Air** - Touchstone Pictures
Director: Simon West
Starring: Nicolas Cage, John Cusack, John Malkovich
Locations: Dead Horse Point SP, Canyonlands NP, Monument Valley, (all were flyovers)

1997 – *Lost Treasurer of Dos Santos* – JCS Entertainment
Director: Jorge Montesi
Starring: David Carradine, Lee Majors, Cathy Lee Crosby, Michele Greene
Locations: Dole/Bates Ranch, Onion Creek, Flat Pass, Mill Canyon, Highway 128, Potash Road

1998 – *Chill Factor** - Morgan Creek Productions/WB
Director: Hugh Johnson
Starring: Cuba Gooding, Jr.
Locations: Monument Valley, Castle Valley, Highway 128

1997 – *The Perfect Getaway* – Bonneville Worldwide Entertainment/ABCTV
Director: Armand Mastroianni
Starring: Adrian Pasdar, Kelly Rutherford, Alicia Coppola, Antonio Sabato, Jr.
Locations: Tusher Canyon, Colorado River, Fossil Point, Dole/Bates Ranch, Culvert Canyon, Gold Bar, Highway 128

1998 – *Galaxy Quest* – Dream Works Studios
Director: Dean Parisot
Starring: Tim Allen, Sigourney Weaver
Location: Goblin Valley SP, Little Wild Horse Canyon

1999 – *Mission Impossible II** - Paramount
Director: John Woo
Starring: Tom Cruise
Location: Dead Horse Point SP

1999 – *Vertical Limit** - Mountain High Productions
Director: Martin Campbell
Starrring: Chris Odonell, Robin Tunney, Scott Glenn
Locations: Monument Valley

2000 – *Critter Gitters** - Watercourse Road Productions
Director: Eric Howell
Starring: Sid Yost and Angel Holliday, a chimpanzee
Locations: Downtown Moab, stage station set

2000 – *Nurse Betty** - Dean River Productions
Director: Robert Vernon
Starring: Pat Hingle, Julie Condra, Wes Studi, Leo Rossi
Locations: Moab, La Sal Loop, Thompson Springs, Arches NP, old Highway 191, Woodside

2001 – *Touched by an Angel ** - Carolin Films/CBS
Director: John Adams (TV series)
Starring: Roma Downey, Della Reese, Mandy Patinkin
Locations: Dead Horse Point SP, off Highway 313

2001 – *(Unnamed India Western)* – (undergoing research)
Director: Jayanth Paranji
Starring: Mayish and others from India, **Tim Norton
Locations: Professor Valley, Pucker Pass Overlook, Long Canyon, Green River Overlook, off Highway 313, Monument valley

2002 – *Goldmember** — Avery Pix/New Line Cinema
Director: Jay Roach
Starring: Mike Meyers, Beyonce Knowles, Michael Caine, Robert Wagner, Mindy Sterling, Fred Savage, Diane Mizota
Locations: Highway 279, Highway 128, Fisher Towers

2002 – *The Hulk** - Universal Pictures
Director: Ang Lee
Starring: Eric Bana, Jennifer Connelly, Cam Elliot, Josh Lucas, Nick Nolte, Paul Herrey, Cara Buono, Todd Tesen
Locations: Arches NP

WHAT HAPPENS BETWEEN MOVIES

Television, Commercials, Videos and Stills

Nearly any night of the week television viewers across America can catch glimpses of the unique rock formations and spectacular vistas in southeastern Utah. These beautiful landscapes are seen as background in commercials, travelogues, documentaries, TV series, or music videos on rock and country channels.

Movies may reflect glamour and excitement, but it is television, in all its program forms, that has given stability to the local film industry. Because of the unusual qualities of area national and state parks, this is also a popular place for travelogues. Documentaries may cover everything from John Wesley Powell's river expeditions to the latest in environmental issues. Televisions series, with segments shot around Moab and Monument Valley, include "Alias Smith and Jones," "MacGyver," "Airwolf," and "Touched by an Angel." Bon Jovi, Clint Black, and others, sang their songs amidst the red rocks in the far country.

TELEVISION COMMERCIALS

In between movies, there is a steady stream of advertising agents and their production crews arriving in southeastern Utah. Their goal: To compliment products with a splash of nature at its best. Over the years literally hundreds of TV commercials have been shot here by film companies from all over the world. Production crews are usually small (10 to 30 people), fast, and efficient. They fit into local accommodations without much strain on the tourist industry and, while passing, give a welcome injection into the economy. When released on the market, area exposure provided through this type of filming is worth millions of dollars in advertising.

Hundreds of miles of roads and highways snake through diversified landscapes in Grand and San Juan counties, attracting companies producing all kinds of foreign and domestic vehicle commercials. The creative souls designing the ad campaigns, however, don't always want seemingly accessible places. In 1963 Chevrolet placed one of its cars, along with a lovely negligee-clad model, on top of Castle Rock (also known as Castleton Tower). The 500 foot spire rises a total of 1,000 feet above the valley floor. The only access to the top for the vehicle was via a helicopter drop.

The model will long remember her experience on this shoot. When it was time to wrap for the day, gusting winds made it unsafe for the helicopter to rescue the lovely lady from her perch. Nights get cold in the desert and her flimsy attire offered little protection. One of the crew was dropped to keep her company throughout the night, and brought along some additional clothing. The two were safely air-lifted down the next morning. This commercial was such a success that Chevy repeated the scenario in 1976 and again in 1985.

Isuzu ad executives were impressed enough to give Castle Rock a try, using David Leisure as the salesman in the piece. Leisure, who had recently broken his ankle and was wearing a cast, was placed on top of the spire between the vehicle and the edge of the sheer cliff. As a safety measure, he was fastened to the Isuzu with unseen rigging - a wise precaution. As the helicopter, with camera, zoomed in to get the shot, the wind generated from the whirling blades nearly pulled him over the edge. The company had made several takes by then, but still wanted to try it again. Leisure, a bit shaken, called it quits. Folks will remember the commercial where he says, "Honest, I drove it up here myself," as the camera pulls back to expose him and the Isuzu atop the pinnacle.

Isuzu on top of Castle Rock as crew preps for commercial shoot. Photo by Frank Mendonca.

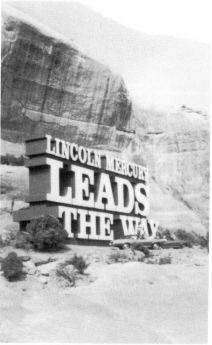

This 1983 Arches National Park set for Federal Express commercial was so convincing that a visitor demanded to know why "Fred" was allowed to build his rock shop within park boundaries.   Courtesy of George White.

A 1970s Lincoln-Mercury commercial shot south of Moab. Courtesy of Marvin Clever.

(Above) Plum Productions used internationally famous rock climber Mike Hoover in 1985 commercial at Dead Horse Point.

(Right) Helicopter delivers giant bottle opener for unique Miller Lite beer commercial filmed at Castle Rock. Photo by Ron Griffith.

Famous Castle Rock has served as the key location for more than just vehicles. HKM Productions filmed a creative commercial in which viewers witness the landmark spire being chipped away to reveal a giant bottle of Miller Lite beer. The concept was fascinating and so convincing that one citizen rushed into the Bureau of Land Management office to find out why this had been allowed to happen.

Over the rim on Miller Lite commercial. Photo by Ron Griffith.

Because of the increase in commercial filming and other small shoots in Grand and San Juan counties, many residents have adjusted their skills to fit the film industry. A good

Chute constructed to launch kayaker off cliff into river for Mountain Dew commercial. Photo by Bego Gerhart.

example is Ron Griffith, who saw a need and filled it. First he purchased a fully-equipped grip truck, then he added a camera van and a motorhome used as an on-set production office, complete with mobile phone and FAX.

Griffith is a specialist when it comes to shooting commercials on whitewater of the mighty Colorado. One project called for the construction of a cable-camera apparatus across the Colorado River in a narrow, rocky, rapid-filled gorge. "What a fun zone this was," said Bego Gerhart. "The idea was to have the camera zing obliquely across the river just as a kayaker plunged toward the camera. Then pow! into the big wave. No problem; four takes, two 'keepers' and a beautiful float downriver to the cars and home." This was a seemingly difficult shoot made relatively easy through the knowledge and skills of local crew.

Camera platform suspended over raging Colorado River for Mountain Dew commercial. Photo by Bego Gerhart.

A production company filming a Diet Mountain Dew commercial wanted a kayak plunging off a cliff in a raging waterfall (where there was NO waterfall) and landing in the rapids below. No problem for Griffith and his production company. Moab's Joe Kiffmeyer, Jose Tejada and Clark Jones joined Ron and Bego in building a chute to launch the kayaker off a cliff overlooking Westwater Canyon rapids. Because it all had to happen in a waterfall, the men rigged a large pump, which was tied onto a river raft and anchored to the cliff face in a churning eddy. They then hosed down the side of the cliff and created the waterfall. "Filming was done from the platform only inches above the surging river, suspended by ropes from the top of the cliff," reports Gerhart. "Most of the ropes were simply tied around huge boulders." When all was set and the cameras rolled, the stunt came off without a hitch.

Fisher Towers, its gigantic spires reaching skyward, provides an excellent commercial backdrop. Resembling those little rocks that grow in the bottom of fish bowls, it was hardly recognizable in a 1993 Jeep commercial. In the bottom-of-the-ocean scenario, a giant stingray and schools of fish are seen swimming past the towers. Suddenly the viewer is brought to the surface to witness the Jeep sitting elegantly on the beach. (The beach was filmed on the California coast).

Toyota television commercial filmed at Fisher Towers in Professor Valley. Photo by Bego Gerhart.

Eggers Films returns often to Moab and Monument Valley for Toyota commercial shoots. One of the most striking was a 1991 project filmed in Professor Valley. Special effects produced mirrored pillars emerging from the ground to reflect the car and Fisher Towers in the background.

An enormous Fisher light was used to highlight a Toyota van in Arches National Park. Photo by B.J. Griffith.

A Peugeot commercial required construction of a fake boulder with an hydraulic lift, a task accomplished by some very creative locals. Larry Campbell, Moab's vehicle fabricator, helped design the prop. The boulder was placed in the center of a stream that feeds water into Kens Lake. In the scene, the car drove onto a platform (bridge), suspended like a tetter-totter over the boulder, then stopped and balanced. The message? Peugeot's perfect balance, of course.

Bego Gerhart often works with the Eggers group and reports that director Tony Phillips and producer Dawn Iacino love to "go over the edge." He explains how he and others help make this happen:

On location with Peter Andrews Productions during filming of Peugeot commercial at Ken's Lake near Moab. Photo by Larry Nagel.

When the camera goes over the edge you better have skilled, dependable crew. Photos show various camera riggings that place film officials in precarious places for spectacular shots. Right photo shows bike wheel used to move a Steadicam up and down the cliff. Photos by Bego Gerhart.

"There is a lot of horizontal vastness in these parts, but some people come to shoot the vertical. With help from local Millie Birdwell, we built speedrail and plywood camera platforms that are suspended down the cliffs by ropes anchored from the top. More 'edgework' for Eggers on yet another Toyota commercial called for a Steadicam rig that could be sent straight down a sheer cliff toward a climber at the top of Long Canyon. Parallels and aluma-beams got us out from the cliff and a bicycle wheel made the rig go up and down. Regardless of how challenging a scene set up might be, safety always comes first."

Filming car commercial, showing the entrance road into Arches National Park. Photo by Bego Gerhart.

Buick about to be dropped into Long Canyon for TV commercial. Photo by Ron Griffith.

Other vehicles seen traveling Utah's canyon country roads on your television screen include: Mitsubishi, Nissan, Honda, Ford, Jeep, Dodge, Plymouth, and Cadillac. Viewers will also see companies selling Conoco, Shell Oil, and other petroleum products, as well as motorhomes, trucking services, and all manner of transportation, with southeastern Utah scenery as backdrop.

167

Conoco commercials filmed in Monument Valley (with set construction) and on the Dolores River crossing. Photos by Jean Akens and Kurt Balling.

Jeep Cherokee commercials filmed on slickrock with rain water reflection (left) and in Onion Creek (right). Photos by Bego Gerhart.

Hyundai commercial filmed by McWaters Films at Castle Rock. Photo by B.J. Griffith.

Set constructed at Woods Cross between Green River and Price, Utah, for Shell commercial. Photo by Ron Griffith.

As for transportation, British Airways filmed one of the most elaborate commercials ever shot in Utah. The segment, produced in canyon country and directed by Hugh Hudson, holds the record for the most extras used on any local film project, including movies. Fifteen-hundred junior and senior high school kids and a few adults made up the cast for this production. Children from Emery, Grand, and San Juan counties were all needed to pull off the Moab segment.

Filmed on a rim near Dead Horse Point State Park, as well as at Lake Powell, Salt Lake City and the Salt Flats, this project was a logistics nightmare. Tam Halling, a production manager from Salt Lake, did a terrific job bringing it all together for the New York based ad agency Saatchi & Saatchi.

At an area near Dead Horse Point the extras formed a huge face that smiled, winked, then turned into a world globe. The 1,500 bodies were used to create the images. To effect this shot, a well-known choreographer, Judy Chabola, was brought in; she trained a core group of about 50 students from the three-county region who were involved in drill teams and dance classes. These experienced performers were the leaders on set. When the company went into production, the choreographer was hoisted high above in a "cherry picker" to issue directions. The POV (point of view) in the commercial was from an airplane swooping down across the face/globe and rim, then out over the awesome canyon.

Payment for extras was handled in a unique way. Schools received $10 per student and the youngsters were able to keep the outfits worn in the commercial. It was a great opportunity for the young people to discover what filming is all about. However, the predominant word to describe the experience was not "exciting," but "boring." As usual, endless hours were spent waiting for just the right sky and cloud formations.

This project had a bonus. The shooting of the commercial was the subject of a film produced at the same time. This piece was shown on British Airlines flights throughout Europe and Africa. The Moab segment was well covered in the film, providing more exposure to the area.

Famous choreographer, Judy Chabola, drilling key students on routine at Monticello High School for British Airways commercial. Photo by Arlene Sibley.

Key extras for British Airways commercial: A Salt Lake model (left) poses with locals Phyllis Bowthorpe and Shannon Lavender Rowe. Photo by George A. Chritton.

Shooting rapids in Westwater Canyon for a TV commercial. Photo by Ron Griffith.

Canyon country has become synonymous with "Marlboro Country." Tommy White, who took over the Colorado River ranch from his father in the Seventies, hosted Marlboro crews for many years. Tommy even became a "Marlboro Man" in some of the shoots, and had a special room in his house dedicated to Marlboro memorabilia.

Following Tommy's untimely death in 1984, the ranch, which had hosted so many films, was eventually sold to Colin Fryer of Salt Lake City. Fryer changed the name from White Ranch to Red Cliff Ranch and constructed a magnificent lodge, providing a permanent home for the movie museum.

It is not uncommon to see more than one company in the area at a time shooting Marlboro marketing pieces. On several occasions, crews from England, Germany and America were all filming Marlboro commercials or still ads simultaneously.

For a number of years, Philip Morris, (Marlboro's parent company), has staged the European Marlboro Silver Cup competition in southeastern Utah. Over a million applicants filed one year, all wanting to come to America to compete. They were screened down to 100, then to 36, who were brought to the United States for the event. The semi-finals are held in the spring and the finals in the fall. The annual event is put together by the "Adventure Team" from Germany. A special camp for participants has been established in Professor Valley at the Doles/Bate Ranch. Contestants operate in teams of two, and are judged on their skills at horseback riding, and piloting motorboats, 4-wheeldrive vehicles and motorcycles.

Moab's Hans Weibel, who speaks fluent German, has served for years as local coordinator for the Adventure Team. Forty to 50 European journalists converge on Moab each year to cover the Silver Cup competition. Again, this is great exposure for the area. The event films are shown all over Europe and account for many of the tourists who visit southeastern Utah each year.

John Ruhl, local helicopter pilot, has for many years worked closely with Marlboro commercial filming and Silver Cup competition. The camp in Professor Valley was alive with action one day when, during a lunch break, Ruhl took flight in his chopper with a huge bucket (used for fire fighting) dangling below. He made a sweep of the Colorado River, filling the bucket, then headed for camp to dump the load. Ruhl targeted the top of the cook shack for the drop, knowing the weight of that much water could be dangerous if it hit a person directly. As water hit the shack, it showered the entire camp. Everyone scattered to find shelter. Few managed but, good sports that they were, all decided it was mighty cooling on a hot day.

A great amount of merchandizing is built into the Marlboro campaigns. This includes a book "The Marlboro Story," based on the Silver Cup competition, and a line of clothing.

Moab's Verle Green in center with four Marlboro men. Courtesy of Verle Green.

Local wranglers working in one of the many Marlboro commercials and ads shot in southeastern Utah each year. Photo by Karl Tangren.

Anti-smoking commercial for France, filmed in Monument Valley, using Marlboro theme. Photo by Bego Gerhart.

Bullseye Steak Sauce commercial, filmed in Professor Valley. Photo by Bego Gerhart.

With the return of Western movies, commercial makers have capitalized on the popular scenario. From Bullseye Steak Sauce to Carefree Chewing Gum, cowboys are telling it like it is. Tommy White, Karl Tangren, Don Holyoak, Verle Green, Harley Bates, Colin Fryer, Pete Plastow and John Hauer are among some of the local wranglers who work with Marlboro and other Western theme commercials. They have a ready resource inventory of livestock, tack, and assorted equipment and gear needed for this type of filming.

One of the most entertaining aspect of working for the Moab to Monument Valley Film Commission is watching the creative storyboards pass through. Every call presents a new challenge. One caller wanted a "bug wrangler." He needed 100 scorpions for his commercial. It was quickly learned that obtaining the creepy-crawlers would be no problem, since men working at the potash plant near Moab had to shake them out of their clothes each night before going home. As it turned out, the thought of 100 scorpions was more than the crew could deal with. They ended up using only one very large dead critter in the scene.

Winston of Europe uses hang glider to sell cigarettes. Photo by Bego Gerhart.

171

On another occasion, an English film company requested a few thousand cocoons and butterflies. This storyboard called for the cocoons to hatch on command when the director called "Action!" The washing machine/dryer being sold in the commercial was to sit in the middle of the desert, demonstrating its smooth, "butterfly" operation. Unfortunately, most of the butterflies and cocoons - flown in from Florida - died before they reached the set. A few remained, however, and fluttered on cue.

Camera mount on horse, used for shooting a commercial with a Western scenario.

There are many commercials filmed in canyon country by foreign companies. This one is for a Japanese vitamin drink called Lipovitan, filmed at the sand dunes off the Ruby Ranch road and at Hauer Ranch on the Colorado River. Photos by Bego Gerhart.

French cigarette commercial, filmed on Musselman Arch off the White Rim trail, using llamas. Courtesy of Canyonlands National Park.

Clairol hair products commercial package, shot at various locations. All Photos by Bego Gerhart.

Clairol model in Arches National Park.

In Audrey McDougald home.

At Canyonlands Bed and Breakfast.

In Monticello wheat field.

At the Apache Motel.

STILL PHOTOGRAPHY

Canyon country is a still photographer's paradise for a variety of reasons. Whether on billboards, brochures, calendars, or print ads, photographs of red rocks, canyons and desert vistas sell products. Many companies initiate print ad campaigns to run simultaneously with their commercials.

Model Carl Hoffer in still-shot for Western English World. Following several shoots in the area, Hoffer and photographer Norm Clausen opened The Cowboy Trading Company in Moab. Photo by Norm Clausen.

The Dugout Ranch, owned and operated by Heidi Redd, is fast becoming a popular location for Western theme projects. The rustic corrals, tack shop and outbuildings make excellent backdrops for clothing ads and catalogues. A company out of South Korea selected the Dugout Ranch as the perfect setting for their Shane jeans campaign in the summer of 1991.

Sometimes still shots are needed by news media or may be used to illustrate books or magazine articles. Such was the case when *The Detroit News* sent their fashion photographer, Donna Terek, to Moab to do a special eight-page section for the paper. Terek shot so many outstanding fashion pictures that editors expanded the project to 16 pages.

Models posed in fancy gowns throughout Goblin Valley State Park, Arches National Park, and the near-ghost town of Cisco. The models strutted their stuff across sand dunes on state land and slickrock on BLM land. To add a little spice to some of the pictures, Terek asked Moab's Larry Campbell to join the Detroit models in a scene or two. Campbell was working as project production manager when he was suddenly plunked among the beauties to contribute some rugged Western flavor. Because it could be interpreted as news coverage, there were no permit fees required, but all land agencies and MFC received nice credits in the article and the film museum received several lovely photographs.

Model poses on Behind the Rocks coral sand dunes, south of Moab. Photo by Donna Terek.

Reminiscent of the surrealistic style of Southwest artist Georgia O'Keefe, model poses in Arches National Park for The Detroit News fashion feature. Photo by Donna Terek.

Using the rustic background of a ghost town to contrast the beauty of the fashions, local Larry Campbell joins models in this shot for The Detroit News. Photo by Donna Terek.

Verle Green lends his rugged look to this scene filmed at the Spanish Valley Trading Post and Feed Store in Moab, for a Toyota brochure. The photograph was given the "poster effect" by computer enhancement. Courtesy of Verle Green.

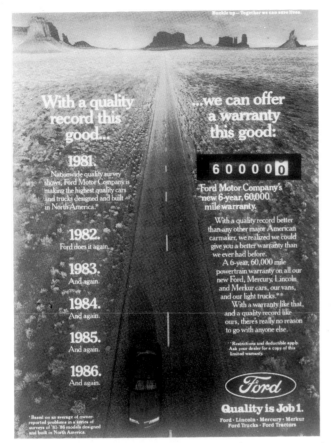

TO CAT... AND CHANGE FOR GOOD

In the seventies, Caterpillar made a tractor appear on the North Mitten in Monument Valley, by using a photo overlay. Courtesy of George White.

This Ford ad appeared in Esquire magazine. The photographer took advantage of the popular, long, straight highway in Monument Valley, Utah.

A sports fashion and fitness special for Bazaar magazine was shot around Moab in 1987.

In addition to Marlboro print-ad campaigns, Camel, Winston, Salem, Lucky Strike and other cigarettes companies have bolstered their brands' popularity with red-rock panoramas. Local model Geno Boyle was selected to become the "Camel Man" in 1991. Later, while on vacation in Europe, he was surprised to be recognized as the Camel Man on the streets of Paris, by a fan who asked for his autograph. Boyle willingly obliged.

The scene that so impressed John Ford, for his first movie in Moab, was used to advertise Skoal. In this ad the photograph was touched up to remove Utah Highway 128, and a camp tent was placed in the picture, far out of scale for the actual scene.

DOCUMENTARIES AND TRAVELOGUES

Numerous documentaries for television and video have been filmed about Native American cultures in southeastern Utah. Other popular subjects include the area's geology, history, and national/state parks. In 1983, Arches and Canyonlands National Parks shared the spotlight in the television special "America the Beautiful." A decade later, Colorado River Adventures filmed a special series for cable distribution about ghost towns, legends, and outlaws. A portion of the series was produced in Grand and San Juan counties. The project was narrated by actor Robert Fuller. The year 1993 also brought Robert Urich to Moab to do a National Geographic Explorer segment, a program he narrates.

Castle Rock has become almost as world famous a landmark as Delicate Arch. In 1984, ABC TV did a documentary for television called "Climbing Castle Rock." This spire is considered one of the outstanding rock climbs in North America.

Robert Fuller teaches Sheri Griffith of Moab to play spoons, during documentary "wrap" party.

Film crews prepare to shoot a piece on Native Americans, with television personality Dave Blackwell (rear). This segment was of Suzie Yazzi and her granddaughter, Loretta, in Monument Valley.

In 1991, Live Stunts Productions selected Moab for one of three stunts for a TV special, "The Greatest Stunts on Earth." Mario Van Peebles narrated the Moab segment. The action: Stuntmen B.J. Worth and Jeff Habberstad were to jump from a helicopter, with B.J. maneuvering a parachute and Jeff hanging onto his legs. At about 125 feet above a landing pad, perched on a point of The Rectory Butte, Jeff would let go and free fall to the pad.

It was November, cold and windy. The company just about had everything ready to shoot when a 90-mile-an-hour wind gust hit. The wooden platform holding the giant air bag erupted into kindling. Undaunted by the misfortune, the company called a two-week break, then returned to rebuild the set.

On the first try of the second round, the wind was blowing just enough to take them off course. Jeff held on to B.J.'s legs until the stuntmen reached the ground at the bottom of the butte. Later in the day, they tried again. This time Jeff was able to maneuver his parachute into position. B.J. dropped, his attention fixed on the target 125 feet below. Falling toward the pad at 60 miles an hour, he managed to land dead center on the large blue-and-white air bag. Everyone breathed a little easier. For additional drama, the bad weather days were also covered in the one-hour special.

Stuntman B.J. Worth, (right) in parachute, drops stunt partner Jeff Habberstad to land on a big airbag, set on the point of a sheer cliff nearly 1,000 feet above Castle Valley.

Air bag landing pad on edge of Rectory Butte, which cushioned a 125 foot fall performed by stuntman Jeff Habberstad. Photos by Bego Gerhart.

MUSIC VIDEOS

Rectory Butte, besides being popular for filming commercials and stunts, is also a great location for music videos. It was there, in 1985, that the rock group Heaven filmed "Knockin' on Heaven's Door." The New Company, producers of the piece, flew the group from New York City to the top of the butte "...in the middle of nowhere." The entire company camped on the high site until the project was completed - which was quite a culture shock for many of them. Local rock climber Eric Bjornstad worked security to guard against any sleep walkers going over the edge. The Company (which had removed the "New" from their name by 1990), returned to film Bon Jovi performing his award-winning "Blaze of Glory" at the same location. This time the storyboard called for an old drive-in movie theater to be constructed on top of the butte, along with placing a few old cars in front of the outdoor screen. In the video, the screen was burned as part of the action.

With the release of "Blaze of Glory" came an outcry from environmental organizations over the set location and burning of the screen in an area with "...such a delicate eco-system." The Grand Canyon Trust sent out a press release condemning the action. Both MFC and the Utah Film Commission were bombarded with complaint calls, based on information in the article. What the article did not explain was the serious controls placed on such film projects, along with the reclamation requirements that follow filming. As a result, the burning of the screen was well-controlled and caused no more damage to the environment than lightning, which often strikes the tops of all buttes in the area. Following production, the site was reclaimed, and BLM personnel concluded that there was little trace that any activity had taken place.

Jon Bon Jovi during filming of "Blaze of Glory" music video, on top of Rectory Butte in Professor Valley.

Members of the rock group Heaven while filming "Knockin' on Heaven's Door," on top of Rectory Butte.

Country and Western singer Clint Black at Wilson Arch, San Juan County. Photo by Bego Gerhart.

Richard Dean Anderson in his role as MacGyver during shoot at Dead Horse Point State Park in San Juan County.

Clint Black used Wilson Arch for his 1992 music video. The arch is located beside U.S. Highway 191 between Moab and Monticello, partly on private land. She Films also produced a video by the group "Sisters" the same year.

The unusual rock formations and breathtaking panoramas make excellent background for music videos. But this segment of the industry has been a bit slower in discovering the potential in canyon country filming. This may be due, in part, to budget limitations, since it is much less expensive to film in a studio.

TELEVISION SERIES

"Alias Smith and Jones" rode into town in 1972 to film the 2-hour pilot for the series. At the same time, filming was done on various segments for several other programs that were seen weekly on television at that time. The key location was a ranch in Castle Valley. Most of the scenes were filmed throughout Castle Valley, Professor Valley, Arches National Park and in the La Sal Mountains.

In 1985, the opening scenes of a 2-hour pilot for "MacGyver" were shot at Dead Horse Point State Park. When it aired on television, it was identified as "Somewhere in Asia," and about 50 Navajos played Mongolian soldiers. In this production, a plane had crashed on the rim of the canyon. Paramount Pictures hauled in the plane wreckage and set it in place at this out-of-the-way location. It was interesting to note that not one pilot flying over the area reported seeing a possible crash during the 15 days of filming.

Numerous scenes for the CBS TV series "Airwolf" were shot numerous scenes in the Monument Valley area, many of which were aerials. Companies producing television series seldom travel to distant locations for their projects because of the cost. If MMVFC lands a series, it will usually be for the pilot movie, which is used to sell the story line to the public and the networks as a continuing series. To date, all of the pilots filmed in the area have proven very successful.

*Joseph Swerling, Jr., producer and director of **Alias Smith and Jones** TV series.*

Stars of **"Alias Smith and Jones"** television series.   Photos from the Bonnie Midlam collection.

Ben Murphy and Bonnie Midlam.

Roger Davis

Frank Sinatra, Jr., James Drury, and J.D. Cannon at the Desert Inn (now the Ramada Inn).

Actor Dean Jagger and Mrs. Jagger.

Character actor, Paul Fix.

Rod Cameron and Bonnie Midlam.

Buddy Ebsen.

Don Holyoak, MMVFC president and long-time movie wrangler, has worked in front of the camera and behind the scenes. Here he is on set for a commercial with a Western theme.

HUMAN RESOURCES

Film people continue to discover what spectacular sets, stunts, and special effects can be achieved in the rugged country of southeastern Utah. The dramatically varied and colorful landscapes, along with today's technology and a talented crew, make for a memorable location experience. An award-winning product can be a bonus for filming in canyon country.

The area's natural resources deserve most of the credit for attracting film companies, but local human resources have certainly given the film commission a competitive edge. Of the 20,000 people residing in the two-county region, many are experienced and talented in film work and support services. For them, working in the film industry has become a way of life.

The number one goal in southeastern Utah is to acquire a diverse and stable economy, while maintaining a quality environment. As actor Jason Patric stated on CBS "This Morning" (following his work on the 1993 movie *Geronimo: An American Legend*): "Moab is one of the most beautiful places on earth." Folks here want to keep it that way, and the film industry is inclined to assist with this goal.

While filmmaking is far from the major livelihood in Grand and San Juan counties, it is a significant contributor to the economy. Film also adds a touch of color to the economic foundation and provides worldwide exposure, enhancing tourism. During hard times, the film industry has been fondly viewed as "the bridge that gets folks across troubled waters."

* * *

The year 1994 marks the 45th anniversary for the Moab to Monument Valley Film Commission. Since 1996 is Utah's Centennial year, residents are in a mood to reflect on things past. Compiling this book for publication has truly been a team effort of the film commission, publisher, involved citizens, and the author. As stories continue to pour in, it has been difficult to bring the project to a close and get it to press.

MMVFC is interested in further developing its Film Museum and Library. If, as some predict, location filming will become obsolete in the 21st century, film history, both oral and written, is needed for MMVFC's museum files.

For every story related in this book, there are many tales yet untold. Reading **"WHERE GOD PUT THE WEST"** should jog a few memories. Residents, movie buffs with something to contribute, as well as others involved in the local film industry, are encouraged to jot down related facts and experiences and submit them to the MMVFC Museum and Library, P.O. Box 61, Moab, Utah, or call for an oral interview (801) 259-6388. Your contributions to area history will be greatly valued and appreciated.

Bette L Stanton

Lucy Carlisle, local makeup artist for film companies since 1975, puts the final touches on James Arness for a television special on John Wayne. The one-hour show, narrated by Arness, was filmed in Monument Valley and at Pack Creek Ranch near Moab.

BIBLIOGRAPHY

1974   THE WESTERN FILMS OF JOHN FORD
        by J.A. Place
        Citadel Press

1984   THE FILM ENCYCLOPEDIA
        by Ephraim Katz
        Perigee Books

1984   LAND OF ROOM ENOUGH AND TIME
        ENOUGH
        by Richard E. Klinck
        Peregrine Smith Books (reprint)

1985   THE OFFICIAL JOHN WAYNE REFERENCE
        BOOK
        by Charles John Kieskalt
        Citadel Press

1986   THE HOLLYWOOD REPORTER
        by Tichi Wilkerson and Marcia Borie
        Arlington House

1987   THE ILLUSTRATED WHO'S WHO OF CINEMA
        by Lloyd Fuller Desser
        Portland House

1987   HALLIWELL'S FILM GUIDE - 6th EDITION
        by Leslie Halliwell
        Charles Scribner's Sons
        MacMillan Publishing

1987   THUNDER IN THE DUST
        by John Calvin Batchelor
        Stewart Tabori & Chang, Inc.

1987   THE WORLD ALMANAC WHO'S WHO OF
        FILM
        by Thomas G. Aylesworth and John S. Bowman
        Bison Books Corporation

1988   DOVE HOLLYWOOD HA CREATO IL WEST
        by Carlo Gaberscek
        Supplemento al n.71 dei
        Quaderni della Face - Udine, Italy

1988   GRIFFITHIANA
        by Carlo Gaberscek
        LaCineteca Del Friuli
        12-21 Ottobre
        The Vanishing American: A Monument Valley
        prima di Ford

1989   TV, MOVIES & VIDEO GUIDE
        by Leonard Maltin
        Signet

1989   THE COMPLETE FILM DICTIONARY
        by Ira Konigsberg
        Meridan

1990   GREAT HOLLYWOOD WESTERNS
        by Ted Sennett
        Harry N. Abrams, Inc.
        A Times-Mirror Company

1993   THE WESTERN
        by Phil Hardy
        William Morrow & Company, Inc.

ARIZONA HIGHWAYS:
1956   April
1981   September
1989   September
1992   January

TIME:
1991   June 24

THE REEL REPORT: Moab Film Commission Annual
Newsletter
1989
1990
1991
1992

INTERVIEWS:
George White - Moab
Mike Goulding - Monument Valley
Essie White - Moab
Jack Goodspeed - Moab
Arnel Holyoak - Moab
Ross "Rusty" Musselman - Monticello
Virginia Johnson - Moab
Marvin Clever - Moab
Ev and Betty Schumaker - Arizona
Eric Bjornstad - Moab
Don Holyoak - Moab
Karl Tangren - Moab
Lin Ottinger - Moab
Carlo Gaberscek - Udine, Italy
Clea Johnson - Blanding
John Hauer - Moab
Bego Gerhart - Moab